BRITISH STEAM ON THE PAMPAS

British Steam on the Pampas

The Locomotives of the Buenos Aires Great Southern Railway

D. S. Purdom

C Eng, FIMechE

Forword by
Andrew B. Henderson, C Eng, FICE, FIMechE
Past Chairman, Railway Division of the
Institution of Mechanical Engineers
Senior Partner, Livesey & Henderson

MECHANICAL ENGINEERING PUBLICATIONS LIMITED
LONDON AND NEW YORK

Typeset by Reproduction Drawings, Ltd., Sutton, Surrey.

Printed and bound by The Burlington Press, Foxton, Royston, Hertfordshire

Foreword

In this world of change much information of historic value and interest in specific fields is liable to be lost or destroyed due to lack of interest and carelessness.

It was therefore a pleasant surprise to hear that Douglas Purdom had written a book on the steam locomotives which had run and in some cases are still running on the old Buenos Aires Great Southern Railway now renamed Ferrocarril General Roca.

Douglas Purdom was an old friend of mine and I had known him since 1939 when he was a very senior member of the mechanical department of the railway and was most helpful and kind to a young engineer with virtually no experience of working overseas. Nothing was too much trouble for him and he would always be prepared, at inconvenience to himself, to help out any young engineers with problems of any sort.

It was, therefore, a great pleasure when his son, Mr Robert Purdom, invited me to write this foreword to his Father's book and I accepted the privilege with alacrity.

On reading this interesting and informative book one reaches a number of definite conclusions in that the steam locomotives could not have run, and some are still running, for more than sixty years if they had not been modified, repaired and maintained by extremely able engineers with complete mastery of their craft and a great dedication to duty.

A great example of an engineer with these two qualities was Douglas Purdom, who during a period of 27 years rose from the position of an assistant engineer to Chief Mechanical Engineer of a railway system of major importance and highly complex to operate, due to many conditions which are completely different to those met in Europe and USA.

He had a most attractive personality and was liked and respected by the

Argentine staff as much as by the expatriate staff. All his qualities were shown to be fully appreciated when the Argentine Railways were nationalized and he was kept as a Chief Mechanical Engineer until he retired in 1951. This period must have been fraught with difficulties, due to many of the trained local staff leaving the railway due to the inevitable political issues that always creep in when a foreign asset is nationalized; as you would expect Douglas Purdom did an outstanding job and the services were kept running.

After reading this book one cannot but help being proud of British engineers and engineering. Of all the locomotives mentioned more than 98 per cent are British built and of the remainder a large proportion were built to British designs.

Speaking from my own time in Argentina, which was unfortunately after the economic problems had set in, all departments on the railway were under strict instructions to spend the absolute minimum, and that the services must be maintained and if possible improved; rather a tall order when it was made clear that the chances of obtaining funds for capital expenditure for new equipment were slim.

Despite these drastic conditions this book shows that a number of locomotives ran for over 60 years and that many steam locomotives are still in service.

The conditions in Argentina vary enormously from one part of the country to another and therefore equipment was required and was developed to suit these local conditions; nowadays oil-firing of steam locomotives is taken for granted and in general does not now cause any major problems and I believe that this can be attributed to the development of a sound and easy to operate system in Argentina. This is merely one of the advances developed by able engineers in order to obtain maximum performance under the local conditions.

I was pleased to see that Douglas Purdom mentioned the development of diesel locomotives and train-sets on the Buenos Aires Great Southern Railway. In the railway world most people believe that all diesel locomotives and trains date from the end of World War II and it is therefore a further tribute to British engineering and design that reliable diesel trains were running in Argentina in 1930.

This is a very excellent book describing an era in which British engineers were able to lead the world and the technical information must be of great interest and value to all engineers.

A. B. HENDERSON

Preface

At the outset this book was intended to be purely a historical-technical record of the locomotives of the BAGSRy, but as work on it progressed the research involved shed more and more light on the multiple activities and ramifications of this remarkable enterprise, the like of which has seldom or never been known in the sphere of British overseas operations. It was felt, therefore, that something of the framework within which this worthy fleet of locomotives operated was called for as a background to the description of their careers and technical characteristics, which in themselves represent a significant chapter in the history of the British locomotive manufacturing industry.

It is for this reason that a fair amount of historical descriptive matter concerning matters not strictly within the purely locomotive sphere has been added: 'trimmings' which it is hoped that those who read this book will consider to be appropriate.

The diesel trials of the early thirties constitute a most important milestone in the history of diesel traction and to the best of my knowledge these have never before been awarded the attention they undoubtedly merit.

It will be noted that the locomotive class diagrams contain no dimensions, which some may consider an unfortunate omission. This was deliberate as I have seen too many similar diagrams so festooned with figures and their corresponding lines and arrows as to make the diagrams as such almost indecipherable. The majority of readers, of course, will require dimensions, so I have quoted the main ones in the text for each class, and for those who wish for fuller details I have prepared the table at the end of the book. This, I hope, will be accepted as a suitable and adequate alternative to the 'Christmas tree' type of diagram.

I should like to place on record my gratitude to Mr L. W. H. Lowther for all his kind help in the revision and presentation of this work and to his belief in this

Preface

work that finally led to its publication. I am also indebted to Mr Richard Campbell of Buenos Aires for having supplied some of the most interesting photographs included in it.

D.S.P.

Contents

1

Introduction

On Leap Year's Day, 29 February 1948, there ended an epoch, the magnitude and significance of which has perhaps never been awarded the importance that it merits in the history of the British Empire and of British industry.

As from midnight on that historic date the British-owned railways in the Argentine Republic ceased to exist as such and became the property of the Argentine government.

The seven railways concerned were four broad gauge (5 ft 6 in), the Buenos Aires Great Southern, the Central Argentine, the Buenos Aires and Pacific and the Buenos Aires Western, two standard gauge, the Entre Ríos and the Argentine North Eastern, and the metre gauge Buenos Aires Midland.

One other metre gauge railway, formerly British-owned, the Central Córdoba, had been nationalized in the year 1936 and merged into the existing Argentine State Railway system, itself predominantly metre gauge.

To complete the nationalization of 1948 three French-owned railways were taken over, the broad gauge Rosario to Puerto Belgrano and the metre gauge Cia. General de Buenos Aires, and Province of Santa Fé lines.

The Province of Buenos Aires Railway, also of metre gauge was at the same time transferred from the ownership of the Province to that of the unified national network.

Conjointly the British-owned railways mentioned constituted the largest British commercial enterprise ever to operate outside the confines of the Homeland or Commonwealth, and as the result of its having existed there accrued enormous benefits to British trade and industry for the best part of a century.

At the same time the impact produced by the British-owned railways on all forms of life and activity in the great republic of the River Plate was indeed profound, and if its men of stature would pause to reflect they would undoubtedly agree that the benefits their country received far outweighed the cost.

They would also be bound to recognize that more than two decades after the passing of the former British organizations, the country still enjoys a worthy heritage from their sojourn, and that the fruits of that heritage will continue to provide benefit for all Argentinians for countless years to come.

It is rather to be regretted that during the negotiations for the transfer, on both sides and particularly in the later stages, the attitude tended to be to look upon the change-over as a rather squalid financial deal and nothing more, and that subsequently a certain amount of rather undignified recrimination, also from both sides, set the keynote for contemporary publicity, overshadowing and obscuring the main point, which was that for the best part of a hundred years the presence of the British-owned railways in Argentina had produced incalculable benefits for both countries.

When one reads the accounts of the ceremonies on the occasion of the cutting of the first sod of the railway, the arrivals of the first trains at Chascomus, Bahía Blanca, Neuquen, Patagones, and other similar events, and sees how in the speeches made by the highest authorities in the land, Presidents, Governors and Ministers vied with one another in lavishing the greatest and most extravagant praise on British enterprise and on the men who carried this out, it is almost incredible and unbelievably sad, that the kind of situation that existed in 1948 could ever have come to pass.

One of the most outstanding aspects of the contribution of British industry to the development of the vast Argentine railway network was undoubtedly in the field of steam locomotive development.

It seems a great pity that no comprehensive records of the achievements in that field were ever compiled at or subsequent to the time of the nationalization, which event at first sight signified the commencement of the gradual eclipse of the steam locomotives by diesels as no new steam locomotives were purchased from then on.

The fact is, however, that nearly twenty years later many British built steam locomotives well over forty years of age were still in active service with their original boilers, and as late as 1968 there was a marked tendency to rely more and more on steam for important services from which it was believed that it had vanished for ever.

At the end of the year 1923 a Paper was read in Buenos Aires by the late Mr John Poole before the South American Centre of the Institution of Locomotive Engineers. Entitled 'Argentine Broad Gauge Locomotive Design' this provided a most excellent and comprehensive record of the subject up to the year in question, and other Papers read before the same Centre from time to time throughout later years dealt with specific features of the design, maintenance and operation of the locomotives, but on the whole the memory of the many fine types of machines involved has faded into obscurity.

There was close contact between the Mechanical Engineers of the various British-owned railways; their problems were to a great extent similar, and as time went on quite a measure of standardization of detail design, maintenance and operating procedures was achieved so that the description of locomotive development on any one railway must have much in common with that on the other railways of the same group.

The present work deals with the locomotive stock of the largest of these railways, the Buenos Aires Great Southern, which in 1926 in its advertisements proudly claimed to be the greatest transportation enterprise in the Southern Hemisphere.

It is an attempt to trace the history and development of the steam locomotives of this railway from 1924 to 1967.

The year 1924 is taken as the starting point for several reasons. First, it carries on from the period covered by Mr Poole's historic Paper already mentioned, and second, because it was in 1924 that the writer joined the Mechanical Department of the BAGSRy and from then on was in a position to observe the locomotive fleet at first hand.

The year 1924 can also be taken as the beginning of the decade during which the British-owned railways reached the peak of their magnificence in all respects, but at the end of which, sad to relate, the writing on the wall was beginning to become visible.

This showed in the form of intensified road competition from the new network of highways, the drain from unfavourable exchange rates which about that time ushered in a long period of increasing inflation and currency devaluation in Argentina, and official support for labour legislation which prevented the most economical deployment and utilization of the staff.

All figures quoted are in accordance with contemporary official records which for this purpose have been coordinated with the personal experience of the author.

Great efforts are being made in Britain today to preserve examples of many outstanding classes of steam locomotives, as well as of some not so outstanding, for sentimental reasons. It probably will not be possible to bring about the preservation of any of the magnificent fleet of over 700 locomotives about to be described, which as a whole, plus nearly 2000 additional locomotives exported to the other British-owned railways in Argentina, represented a goodly proportion of the output of the British locomotive industry during the first third of this century.

Assuredly, however, they have earned some kind of memorial, even if it be merely in the form of the text and photographs of this modest attempt to outline their history.

2

Description of the BA Great Southern and Associated Railways and their Train Services

In 1937 there was published in Buenos Aires, in Spanish, a book of truly remarkable historical interest entitled *Historia del Ferrocarril Sud 1861-1936* (History of the Southern Railway 1861-1936). It was written by William Rogind, who was born in Denmark in 1861 and first arrived in Buenos Aires in 1890. A year later he entered the Civil Engineering Dept. of the Southern Railway as a draughtsman and surveyor. In 1930 he retired from the post of Assistant Chief of the Drawing Office, dedicating much of his time thereafter to the preparation of his book. Unfortunately he did not see it published, as he died in April 1935, the finishing touches being given to the work by some of his former colleagues who had collaborated with him in the earlier stages.

The book consisted of 59 chapters occupying 692 large pages and was profusely illustrated with photographs, engravings, maps, and diagrams, the latter being Mr Rogind's own work. It was a remarkable book for two main reasons, first for the enormous amount of factual information it contained, much of which is probably not recorded anywhere else, and second, for the manner in which it demonstrated without a shadow of doubt that the history of the region traversed by the Southern Railway was in effect the history of the railway itself.

In 1861 the first steps were taken towards obtaining a concession to build the line of 114 km from Buenos Aires to Chascomús, the originator being Mr Edward Lumb of Liverpool, later resident in Argentina.

Official authorization was granted in May 1862 and the following month the corresponding contract was signed between the Argentine Government on the one hand and Mr Lumb on the other. In due course Mr Lumb was able to interest a number of influential British business and railway men and the Buenos Aires Great Southern Railway Company was formed.

The Board of Directors in London was composed as follows:

Mr John Anderson—a Director of the South Eastern Railway
Mr J. P. Brown MP—Vice Chairman of the London and North Western Railway
Mr John Fair—Argentine Vice-Consul in London
Mr Charles Gilpin MP—a Director of the South Eastern Railway
Mr J. A. H. Holt—formerly of Bromwell and Co. of Buenos Aires
Mr Jose Rivolta—of A. Rivolta and Sons, London
Mr David Robertson MP
Mr William Scholefield MP
Mr H. A. Wilkinson—Chairman of the Metropolitan Railway

There were thus four Members of Parliament and four Directors of British Railway Companies included.

The Directors in Buenos Aires were as follows:

Mr Frank Parish HM Consul in Buenos Aires
Mr Edward Lumb

The first General Manager was Mr Edward Banfield whose name is now borne by one of the busiest suburban stations.

The original capital of the new company was £750 000.

It should be borne in mind that at this period Argentina was torn by civil conflict and internal dissension. The tyrant Rosas had only recently been finally defeated at the battle of Caseros and most of the territory beyond the point to which the new railway was to penetrate was still under the domination of the savage Indian tribes. It was not surprising therefore that Mr Lumb's original efforts to raise the necessary capital in Buenos Aires met with no response. On the other hand it says much for the farsightedness and spirit of adventure of the gentlemen in London who supported this enterprise, which in the course of time developed into such a brilliant success. This, sad to say, is in direct contrast to the vacillating and timid attitude so often in evidence in later years which has signified for Britain the loss of so much overseas trade to foreign competitors.

On 7 March 1864 the first sod of the bed of the new railway was cut by the President of Argentina, General Bartolome Mitre, on the site of the present terminus at Plaza Constitución in Buenos Aires, and the line as far as Chascomús was completed on 14 December 1865, there being at first nine intermediate stations. The rolling stock consisted of 8 small tank engines, 38 carriages and 184 wagons.

Acknowledgement is hereby given to Mr Rogind's book for the foregoing information which is considered of sufficient historic interest to warrant its inclusion, though the present work in no way claims to be a complete history of the railway.

To jump as it were to the other end of the scale, its tremendous development over 64 years can be judged from the following statistics for the financial year 1929/30.

Kilometres of track open	8061
Number of stations	504
Total staff	33 409
Number of locomotives	857
Number of carriages	955
Number of wagons	16 602
Number of passenger trains run	285 229
Number of passengers carried	60 509 600
Tons of freight transported	8 272 730
Capital in pounds sterling	82 780 760
	(110 times that of 1865!)

The year in question marked the peak of the railway's prosperity and it was during the second half of 1930 that the first ill effects of the crippling blow caused by the progressive devaluation of the Argentine peso began to be felt.

In the twelve months from June 1930 to June 1931 the value of the peso declined by 22 per cent which not only meant that profits remitted to London were reduced by 22 per cent, but the prices of all imported fuel, supplies, and materials were increased by a like amount.

Simultaneously the liberalization of labour legislation brought about substantially increased costs under that heading, but little or no relief in the form of increased tariffs was permitted, while in any case competition from transport on the rapidly expanding network of metalled roads was already making matters more difficult.

It can safely be said, therefore, that the year 1930 saw the commencement of the process which finally led to the sale of the British owned railways eighteen years later.

To give some idea of the overall influence of the Southern Railway within its sphere of operation mention should be made of the numerous ancillary services owned and operated by the company itself or by subsidiary and associated companies.

The moles and grain elevators at Ingeniero White and Puerto Galvan in the Bahía Blanca port area, together with the necessary tugs, barges, launches, etc.

The electric power station at Loma Paraguaya, Bahía Blanca.

The South Dock moles and sheds.

The moles and sheds at Rio Santiago near La Plata.

The experimental fruit farm at Cinco Saltos in the Rio Negro valley.

The Argentine Fruit Distributors company.

The agricultural light railways at Balcarce and elsewhere.

The Condor long distance omnibus company.

Up to the time of the 1914–18 war the company owned several small ocean going steamers which were used mainly for bringing coal and other supplies from Britain, returning with Argentine produce of various kinds.

The company built and for a time operated a hotel at Sierra de la Ventana, and in later years built a comfortable hotel with adjoining golf course at Miramar which was administered by the Restaurant Department.

Together with the other British-owned railways the Southern had an interest in the 'Compania Ferrocarrilera de Petroleo' in Comodoro Rivadavia whose wells supplied a considerable proportion of the oil fuel used on those railways.

From the foregoing one can realize what a vast enterprise the Southern Railway became and how great an influence it exercised on the life and development of the Province of Buenos Aires.

This province ranks first in the country as a producer of livestock and only second to Santa Fé as a producer of grain. It is a vast alluvial plain with stone or rock showing at a few points such as the Tandil, Balcarce, and Ventana hills, with little or no material easily available for the construction of all-weather roads, and until comparatively recent times such roads were few and far between.

The original objective of the railway, therefore, was twofold, first, to provide a reliable means of communication between the towns of the interior and the capital, and second, to enable the produce of the interior largely destined for export and therefore the life-blood of the nation to be transported to the ports.

Map A shows how the Southern lines formed a network in the truest sense of the word throughout the province, and how every part of the area was gradually covered by an easily accessible railway connection.

In recent years much ill-informed and irresponsible criticism of the early policy of the railways has appeared in the press and elsewhere. It is alleged that the construction of lines radiating from the ports has omitted direct intercommunication between towns in the interior which in later years have seen considerable commercial and industrial development. The point is entirely ignored that if each of these

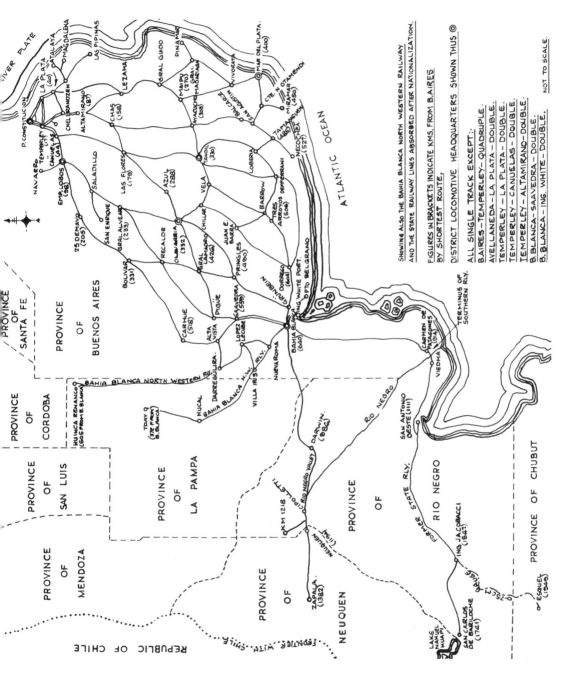

Fig. A Map of Buenos Aires Great Southern Railway

towns had not first been provided with direct access to the capital and the ports, this commercial and industrial development could never have come about. One of the major problems with which the Southern and other railways had to contend was the seasonal nature of much of their traffic.

The movement of wheat, oats, maize, linseed, and other grains was usually concentrated between the beginning of the harvest in December and the following month of May with the object of disposing of the crop before the commencement of the corresponding harvest in the Northern Hemisphere.

The important fruit traffic from the Rio Negro valley consisting mainly of apples, pears, and grapes and which by 1950 had reached a volume of half a million tons, had all to be placed in the cold storage premises in the ports of Buenos Aires and Bahía Blanca between January and March. This traffic was carried in ventilated wagons on passenger train timings and the shipments to Buenos Aires which were by far the greater proportion, involved a journey of nearly 1200 km or 750 miles.

On top of all this the summer tourist traffic to Mar del Plata, Miramar, and Necochea was concentrated within the holiday period from mid-December to mid-March.

It can be appreciated, therefore, that the demand for motive power was far from uniform throughout the year and that consequently any figures of average monthly mileage of the locomotive stock as a whole would be entirely misleading.

Apart from a basic all year round timetable of booked goods trains, much of that traffic was necessarily worked as specials depending from day to day on the actual demands.

It often happened, for example, that during very dry spells in some parts of the province there were large-scale movements of livestock to other zones not so affected where pasturage was still good. This class of traffic, of course, depended entirely on the time and the prevailing circumstances.

As regards goods traffic in general, there was naturally a large proportion of empty wagon movement due to its one-way nature, which could not fail to have repercussions on the tariffs.

In so far as passenger train services were concerned, apart from the Buenos Aires suburban services dealt with in the next chapter and the light suburban services around Bahía Blanca shown on map C, the main flow was from Buenos Aires to Bahía Blanca and beyond by three routes, the direct line via Las Flores, Olavarria and Pringles, a variant of that from Olavarria through General La Madrid and Saavedra, and a third route via Las Flores and Tres Arroyos.

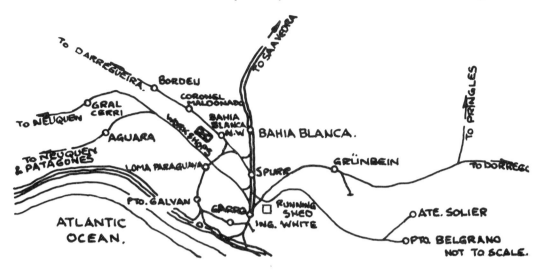

Fig. C Details of lines in Bahia Blanca District

The services beyond Bahía Blanca to Zapala and on the former state railway to Bariloche which at first were served by through carriages on the Bahía Blanca trains soon developed to the point where it became necessary to run separate complete trains to and from Buenos Aires.

Other main line services on a smaller scale were those from Buenos Aires via Bolivar to Carhué, via Maipú to Tandil, via Chas and Ayacucho to Necochea, and the services from Bahía Blanca to Huinca Renanco and to Toay respectively. The branches and connecting lines on all these routes were served either by through carriages or suitable connections.

From its nature the Mar del Plata line was in a somewhat different category in that it carried a heavy service of purely tourist traffic during three months of the year and to a lesser degree during the rest of the year. In addition to the trains serving the intermediate stations there were a number of through expresses which did not pick up or set down passengers at any of these points.

On parts of this line the maximum speed permitted was 120 km/h whereas on most of the other main lines the limits were from 80 to 100 km/h, with 60 to 75 km/h on the more lightly constructed secondary and branch lines.

Apart from the summer holiday trains all other main line trains carried a considerable load of parcels traffic, comprising anything up to half a dozen separate vehicles. Times of intermediate station stops were arranged to cover the corresponding loading and unloading work, but in practice these times often proved insufficient, so the making up of lost time was a common occurrence.

The lines being for the most part single track, out-of-course delays at crossing points were unavoidable at times, and here again time recovery often took precedence over the strict observance of speed limits.

Train loads, particularly on the Bahía Blanca line were heavy and often exceeded 700 tons. In winter, in addition to the actual load, the not inconsiderable resistance of anything up to a dozen heavy generators for electric heating in the carriages had to be overcome, so altogether the standard of locomotive performance called for was of a high order.

Until the automobile and the omnibus became firmly established in the field, overnight travel by train was very popular. For those who could afford the supplement, comfortable sleeping cars with two or four berths were available. Apart from the saving of time, night travel in summer was preferred by many, as the hot daytime sun could make conditions somewhat trying.

Restaurant car facilities were also from necessity supplied on a large scale due to the length of the average journey.

As a matter of interest, in the year 1930 out of a total of 955 carriages, 154 were sleeping cars and 66 were restaurant cars, these two types amounting to 23 per cent of the total.

In the working timetables there figured severe speed restrictions at certain points on the line 'during and after strong winds'. This very necessary precaution was due to the sandy nature of the surroundings where it happened from time to time that sand was blown on the track to an extent which could have caused the derailment of a train travelling at speed.

Other hazards which existed included the frequent presence of stray animals on the track and the possibility of collisions at the many unprotected level crossings. The fitting of powerful electric headlights on the locomotives from 1928 onwards helped matters considerably.

As more powerful locomotives became available the weight of the goods trains gradually increased and with the advent of the three cylinder 4-8-0 class 11C they often reached 2000 tons and over during the harvest season. The Garratts of class 14 could and often did handle trains of even greater weight. The principal limiting factors, in fact, were the capacity of some of the passing loops and the strength of the existing type of wagon draw gear.

These notes of a historical and general nature have been compiled in order to provide the reader with a picture of something of the background within which the locomotives to be described later had to operate and to give an idea of some of the difficult conditions with which they had to contend.

3

The Buenos Aires Suburban Services

The Buenos Aires suburban lines in their present physical form date from 1926 in which year the quadruplication of the tracks as far as Temperley was completed. As can be seen from the sketch map B the network consisted of one main stem as far as Altamirano, 87 km from Buenos Aires on the main line to Mar del Plata, a stem to the West as far as Cañuelas 64 km from Buenos Aires, and a stem to the East along the South bank of the River Plate to La Plata, 40 km from Buenos Aires. From Temperley a connecting line ran to Villa Elisa on the La Plata line and from Bosques on that connecting line a link through Berazetegui enabled circle line trains to run from Plaza Constitución via Temperley and back via Berazetegui and Quilmes and vice versa.

The single line showing a connection from Coronel Brandzen on the Altamirano line to Ringuelet on the La Plata line runs through open country and is in no sense a suburban line.

The Western Railway ran a few passenger trains from Haedo on the parent system to Marmol, just beyond Temperley, but the main purpose of this connecting line was the very considerable livestock traffic from the Western Railway zone to the large meat packing plants at Berisso, just outside La Plata from which point the produce for export was loaded direct on to the ocean going ships.

Though from the traffic working point of view the three outermost stations mentioned, Altamirano, Cañuelas, and La Plata marked the limits of the respective suburban services, in actual fact many trains terminated short of these destinations. On the centre, or main line there were trains which terminated at Remedios de Escalada, Temperley, Burzaco, Glew, and San Vicente.

In the earlier years most of the trains on the Cañuelas line originated at Temperley and were usually of light formation with class 8C engines in charge.

Those on the Temperley to La Plata line and on the circle line were mostly of similar make up.

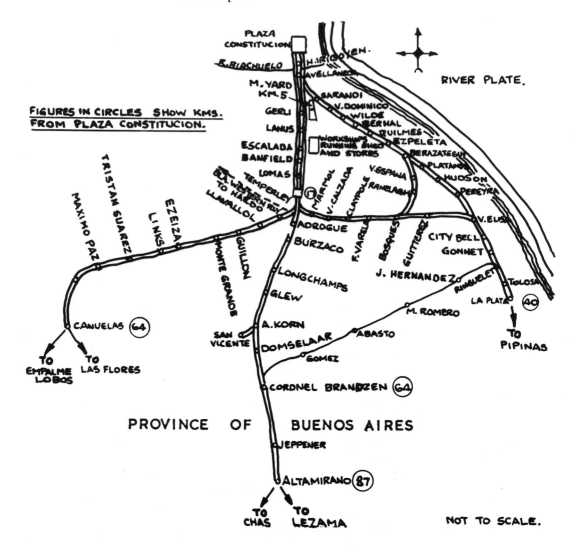

Fig. B Buenos Aires suburban lines

On the La Plata line many trains terminated at Quilmes or Berazategui, although with La Plata being the capital city of the Province of Buenos Aires there was always a heavy through traffic. This 40 km run was frequently made non-stop and the principal trains had a restaurant car attached.

Until in 1930 the class 8E engines were permitted to run over the strengthened viaduct at Sarandí, this direct La Plata service was one of the heaviest with which the smaller class 8C engines had to cope.

Of the many important works in the programme which began in 1922, the most imposing was the reconstruction of the terminal at Plaza Constitución. The foundation stone of the new main building was laid by HRH the Prince of Wales (later the Duke of Windsor) on 19 September 1925 during his official visit to Argentina. As reconstructed this station has fourteen platforms roofed over, modern hydraulic buffer stops and the usual crossovers etc, at the inner ends. A magnificent well lighted concourse forms a huge hall along the whole width of the site.

The plan provided for priority being given to the operating part of the station, i.e. the platforms, approach lines, signalling, etc, followed by the construction of the concourse. Over the space between the concourse and the platform-ends a six storey office block was built, which was carried round the East end to the front street.

Also to the East of the main station a spacious and well equipped goods and parcels section with warehouses, offices and several sidings was built and brought into service.

There remained the main street frontage, to be formed by a further block of offices and which, had it been completed, would have been one of the most imposing buildings in the city. Unfortunately when the time came for this phase of the job to be tackled financial conditions in general had begun to deteriorate and it was reluctantly decided to leave it in abeyance, which is still the situation fifty years later. Happily, however, the original frontage of the station, dating from 1885 had remained untouched, and being of pleasing architecture it harmonized very well with the new part.

Internally the office accommodation was modernized and in actual practice the lack of the anticipated additional office space was never felt, at least for as long as the railway remained in private hands.

Of the fourteen platforms only two or three were normally used by mainline trains, leaving eleven for the suburban services.

Other important works in the overall programme included the installation of automatic signalling for the approaches to the terminus, extending out to the junction with the La Plata line at Avellaneda, and automatic signalling between Km 12 and Temperley. These installations were manufactured and installed by the Westinghouse Brake and Signal Co. of London.

The quadruplication of the tracks as far as Km 12 had been completed in

1912 and its prolongation as far as Temperley, 17 km from Plaza Constitución, was begun in 1922 and completed in December 1925. This work included the construction of handsome and spacious new stations at Banfield, Lomas, and Temperley which after fifty years can still be considered as outstanding examples of station architecture.

The existence of a large number of level crossings on the suburban lines has always been a source of considerable inconvenience and though many projects for the construction of overbridges or underground passages have been drawn up, very little progress has been made to date due to difficulties which have nothing to do with the railway.

To give some idea of the volume and density of the suburban traffic, some authoritative figures for the year 1925 will first be quoted.

On 6 December 1926 the *Railway Gazette* published the second of two special South American numbers. This contained an article entitled 'The Suburban Traffic of Buenos Aires' by the same William Rogind who was the author of the history of the Southern Railway mentioned in the previous chapter. With due acknowledgement of the source the following figures from the article in question are given below. These figures correspond to the year 1925 and refer to the traffic on the 90 km with 36 stations comprising the following sections:

> Plaza C to Longchamps
> Avellaneda to Berazategui
> Temperley to Bosques, Ranelagh and Berazategui
> Temperley to Tristan Suarez

Daily number of suburban trains despatched from Plaza C.—167 ⎱ 336
Daily number of suburban trains received at Plaza C.   —169 ⎰
Total suburban traffic for year 1925 in passengers—43 319 513
Number of passengers dealt with at Plaza C. station—40 135 000

The daily numbers of trains dealt with at the principal suburban stations were as follows:

> Temperley—166
> Burzaco—106
> Lomas—130
> Lanus—113
> Quilmes—117
> Berazategui—72
> Longchamps—53
> Monte Grande—53
> Tristan Suarez—43

These, then, were the principal statistics for the year 1925. Up to the end of that year only twenty-seven of the large class 8E tank engines had been delivered, so on them plus the forty-one class 8C and part of the thirty-four class 8A tank engines fell the brunt of the considerable traffic then existing, including the outer suburban and La Plata services. For a number of years thereafter traffic continued to increase but apart from thirty-four additional class 8E engines no other substantial relief was forthcoming until the arrival of a number of Drewry railcars in 1938 which took over a number of the lighter services radiating from Temperley and La Plata. The five diesel-electric train sets placed in service in 1930 and 1933 did, however, play a full part up to the limit of their capacity.

It was during this period that Plaza Constitución with an annual movement of well over 40 000 000 passengers ranked only second to Liverpool Street, London, with around 76 000 000 passengers annually, as the largest steam operated suburban service in the world, and for some years after the first electrification into Liverpool Street until the large-scale introduction of diesel haulage on the Southern Railway in 1962, the suburban services of the latter were undoubtedly the most intense of any worked by steam in the whole world.

Subsequent to 1925 competition from road transport began to affect the shorter distance suburban services quite seriously, but on the other hand the gradual expansion of the more outlying districts called for more and heavier trains to serve them adequately.

As an example the number of trains from Plaza Constitución which terminated at Remedios de Escalada was reduced considerably, while many services beyond points such as Burzaco, Monte Grande, and Florencio Varela which had previously been covered by light connecting trains, had to be provided with heavy through trains.

The carriages employed on the suburban services were, as described in a later chapter, constructed in the Remedios de Escalada workshops. From about 1923 the latest models were no less than 82 ft long over buffers, with 100 seats in a first class carriage and 150 seats in a second class one. The tare weights varied from 40 to 43 tons so the ten coach formations weighed over 400 tons without passengers. The most numerous formations were of eight carriages and there were a few of five carriages.

With close spacing between stations the locomotive working had to be smart and the repeated accelerations called for an all-out effort.

Oil fuel was used exclusively on these services even during the difficult period of the 1939–45 war and the class 8E's were treble-crewed over the period from 4 a.m. to 2 a.m. on the following day.

Some years after nationalization the situation deteriorated until it became really chaotic. As maintenance declined delays and failures became more frequent, and train formations were reduced as fewer carriages were available. With the consequent overcrowding it became a physical impossibility to inspect tickets properly on the trains with the result that free travel for a time became the order of the day and added still more to the overcrowding.

It was only after 1962 with the purchase of a large number of diesels and of new all steel carriages that a semblance of order and normality could be restored.

Through all those trying times, however, the thirty-year-old class 8E engines, in spite of neglect and poor maintenance, showed their sterling quality and as mentioned later some of them in 1967 were still performing efficiently the duties for which they were originally intended.

It may well be asked why no electrification was carried out on lines of such density of traffic, particularly as both the Western and Central Argentine Railways had electrified their suburban lines with conspicuous success soon after the end of the 1914–18 war. The fact is that considerable thought had indeed been given to this matter, but during the period in question when conditions for going ahead with it were most favourable, the Southern Railway was very heavily involved in other capital works and was not in a position to face this additional capital outlay. When these other works were nearing completion the question of diesel-electric traction was coming under study and in due course the experimental units described in Chapter 12 were built and placed in service with highly encouraging results.

To have been at all comprehensive the Southern electrification would have been considerably larger than that of the other two railways mentioned and as the existing power plants would not have provided sufficient power, at least one additional power station would have had to be built, which in itself would have added enormously to the overall cost.

The respective protagonists of the diesel-electric and straight electric systems produced voluminous reports and statistics over the years tending to demonstrate the advantages of each, but the sad fact is that before any clear-cut decision was arrived at the financial situation of the railway had so deteriorated that large-scale investment on either system was out of the question.

The later diesel-electric powerhouse trains in particular rendered excellent service and their performance certainly constituted a good case for an extension of that system.

From 1930 all new suburban carriages were built with bogies arranged for taking traction motors with the idea of their future adaptation for either system.

At the same time comprehensive studies of electrification were carried out and a scheme was prepared in considerable detail, including the laying of two additional tracks between Plaza Constitución and Avellaneda, and the raising of the platforms at all the stations likely to be served by electric trains.

Subsequent to nationalization the authorities developed several schemes on similar lines, latterly on the basis of the 25 kV a.c. system as used in Britain and elsewhere, and at the time of writing the position is that a cut and dried overall proposal exists, but that financial considerations have so far prevented its being put into effect.

In the meantime the trains are hauled mainly by diesel-electric locomotives, some of which are of powerful main-line classes which could be more usefully employed elsewhere, but it is seldom that at least one daily diagram is not entrusted to the evergreen class 8E steam engines.

4

Mechanical Department—
History and Organization

In 1925 the Southern Railway took over the working of the Bahía Blanca North Western Railway from the BA Pacific Railway.

This involved the transfer from the Pacific Railway of the Bahía Blanca Workshops, the grain elevators at Puerto Galvan and a number of locomotives as detailed under the headings corresponding to each class in a later chapter.

The Southern Railway main workshops were at Remedios de Escalada, or Escalada, as they were generally termed, 11 km out from the Plaza Constitución terminus. The larger running sheds such as Ingeniero White (Bahía Blanca) and Tolosa (La Plata) were equipped to deal with major running repairs.

The extensive grain elevators at Ingeniero White called for the establishment of a small workshop there for maintenance purposes and there were similar facilities for maintenance of the installations at South Dock, Buenos Aires.

The vehicle inspection staff throughout the line consisting of about 400 men also formed part of the Mechanical Department, as did the weighbridge maintenance section.

In 1933 the administration of the Southern, Western, and Midland (metre gauge) lines was combined, but generally speaking, locomotive maintenance procedure was not affected thereby.

This state of affairs continued until shortly after nationalization in 1948 when the Southern became the General Roca Railway, absorbing at the same time the former State Railway lines from Patagones to Bariloche and Ingeniero Jacobacci to Esquel, the latter being of 75 cm gauge.

The Southern half of the former French-owned Rosario to Puerto Belgrano Railway was at the same time absorbed by the Southern.

The Western Railway, under its new name the Domingo Faustino Sarmiento Railway, retained its former autonomy and took over from the Southern two stretches of the Bahía Blanca North Western system, those from Darregueira to Huinca Renancó and from Villa Iris to Toay.

The Midland Railway was absorbed by the former State Railway metre gauge system now known as the General Belgrano Railway.

Over the period covered by this record there were changes of jurisdiction from time to time affecting the running shed staff and the footplate staff.

The following table shows these changes.

	Workshops	*Running sheds*	*Footplate staff*
1924–36	Mechanical Dept.	Mechanical Dept.	Mechanical Dept.
1936–39	Mechanical Dept.	Mechanical Dept.	Operating Dept.
1939–47	Mechanical Dept.	Operating Dept.	Operating Dept.
1947–51	Mechanical Dept.	Mechanical Dept.	Mechanical Dept.

All that need be said regarding these changes is that the separation of locomotive running maintenance from the control of the Mechanical Dept. was not a success.

In 1924 the Chief Mechanical Engineer was Mr P. C. Saccaggio under whose direction most of the modern Southern Railway engines were designed and built.

He was responsible for many innovations of detail design, workshop methods, etc, and also for the construction in the Escalada Workshops of the whole of the modern carriage stock. These vehicles were truly of indigenous manufacture, the wooden bodies and furnishings being produced right from the log and the steel underframes, bogies, etc. from imported plates and sections. Only items such as wheels and axles, springs, brake cylinders, and train lighting equipment were purchased outside.

Commencing in 1929, Mr Saccaggio's pioneer work on diesel electric traction was outstanding, and although this history deals mainly with the railway's steam locomotives, a special chapter about his historic prototype diesel designs is called for, as undoubtedly at the time they were ahead of any similar developments elsewhere.

What must strike any student of locomotive history is the large percentage of outstanding personalities who from time to time have ruled over the various railway Mechanical Departments in Britain and elsewhere throughout the years.

On practically every count, Mr P. C. Saccaggio, of Italian birth but resident in Argentina from childhood, deserves to be included in any list of such notables. It would be no injustice to either party, in fact, to describe him as a super Dugald Drummond. He literally dominated everyone with whom he came in contact, from the humble labourer to the General Manager and Board of Directors, and generally was able to come out on top in any brush with such formidable opponents as the Accountants.

He drove everyone hard, but no harder than he drove himself, and as can be seen throughout this narrative he had evolved a host of most ingenious and useful improvements to his steam locomotives and other rolling stock before dedicating himself to his experimental work on diesel traction.

His command of the English language in all its manifestations was possibly unique, and both his talks with his seniors up to Board level, and his dressing-down of some wretched junior left nothing to be desired.

It was something of a trial, but at the same time a great privilege, to have worked closely with him.

When the centralized administration of the Southern, Western and Midland Railways was formed in 1933 Mr Saccaggio retired, having already passed the usual age limit, and was succeeded by Mr J. W. H. Rea, the then Chief Mechanical Engineer of the Western Railway, though he continued to act as Consultant for diesel traction.

Mr Rea was unfortunate in that by the time he took over the days of lavish capital expenditure on new equipment were over, but nevertheless he was able to produce the excellent 12G, 12H, 12K, and 15A classes. He also produced the class 12F by converting ten class 12 compounds to simple, and in addition by modifications to cylinders, motion, blast arrangements, etc, he made notable improvements to the classes 12A, 12D, and 12E.

Mr Rea retired in 1939 and was succeeded by Mr J. Mailer who had previously been Chief Mechanical Engineer of the British owned Central Cordoba Railway until after it was nationalized in 1936.

His previous experience of having to do a lot with very little stood him in good stead during the wartime and post-war period of financial stringency and virtual paralysis of the importation of spares of every kind, and the railway had every reason to be grateful to him for the excellent condition in which the engines and rolling stock were maintained in the face of almost insuperable difficulties.

After the war ended he was instrumental in having the order placed for the thirty mixed traffic engines class 15B which were later to prove a veritable god-send to the railway.

In August 1947 Mr Mailer retired on pension and his place was taken by Mr P. W. Dobson, who since 1933 had retained the post of Chief Mechanical Engineer of the Midland Railway, acting in addition as Mr Mailer's deputy.

Mr Dobson had barely assumed command when in March 1948 the government took over control and there commenced a period of unimaginable difficulties of all kinds. Being qualified for pension he decided to retire in October 1948 and the writer, as his principal assistant, was appointed to succeed him, being thus the only member of the British contract staff to be appointed to a post of chief officer by the Argentine authorities subsequent to nationalization.

At first, happily, the situation was greatly eased by the fact that there were still competent British staff in many of the key posts; also there was a very competent nucleus of young enthusiastic Argentine technicians who for some time past had been gradually trained for taking over senior posts in due course.

Nevertheless the position as regards motive power was quite serious and before long the establishment of a typical bureaucratic system of purchasing spares and supplies in general, usually on the basis of price alone without reference to quality or durability, made matters even more difficult.

There were moments, in fact, when serious dislocation of the services was narrowly avoided. The purchase of poor quality water level gauge glasses, axlebox waste, rubber buffer springs or rubber neck rings for vacuum brake cylinders was directly responsible for this state of affairs. In the workshops and runnings sheds the use of inferior quality files, drills, paint brushes, etc, caused much trouble. Unfortunately many of these and other doubtful items came from concerns of a fly-by-night nature, which after one good killing were apt to fade away and could not therefore be called properly to account.

In order to ease the motive power situation at this time several modifications were carried out with such material as was available, and these are referred to under the notes on classes 7B, 8A, 11S, 12A, 12K, 12P, respectively, but the progress of this work was seriously handicapped by having at the same time to cope with a full programme of normal repairs with no extra staff and with labour regulations being further relaxed almost daily with the consequent adverse effect on productivity.

As time went on the gradual exodus of the remaining British contract staff accelerated and at the same time the authorities committed their greatest blunder by waging a campaign for supposedly political reasons against most of the competent Argentinians who had been trained for taking over the reins just at this particular moment.

The loss of this able and loyal contingent of technical men was a sad blow for the future efficiency of the railway and nearly twenty years later the effects were still clearly apparent. Happily most of them were received with open arms by private industry where they were much better off.

The gradual infiltration of the key posts in the department by second-rate individuals with political influence during three years brought things to the point where the writer felt it was physically impossible to keep things going in a systematic and orderly manner, and a somewhat serious breakdown in health provided the pretext for retirement in April 1951, albeit with some reluctance to leave an organization after over twenty-seven years of service in it, but the cost of carrying on what was later clearly seen to be a losing battle against bureacracy was too high.

As the author did not become Chief of the Mechanical Department until after the last steam locomotives had been ordered, he did not have the satisfaction of producing any new designs as such, but fortunately he was able to carry out a programme of modernization of several existing classes as mentioned earlier in this chapter and described in greater detail under the respective class headings.

As already noted, this work had to be carried out with little or nothing available in the way of new materials other than what was already available in Stores, and it was further handicapped by the general disorganization which then prevailed.

On the other hand, this same disorganization made it possible to go ahead without seeking higher authority, with all the attendant delay and general frustration, and the various modifications were only made known when they had been completed. As the results were satisfactory, no adverse criticism was forthcoming.

Before concluding this chapter it is only right to place on record the notable work in connection with locomotive design carried out by Messrs T. J. Durnford, F. Gee, J. Poole and R. Phillips, whose joint contribution to the creation of a fleet of outstandingly successful engines was of the greatest merit.

5

Mechanical Department—
Workshops and Running Sheds

Locomotive shop maintenance was carried out chiefly in the main workshops at Remedios de Escalada, 11 km out from Plaza Constitución on the main line. These workshops were originally built in 1901 and by 1924 their capacity for physical expansion was practically exhausted as they were bounded on the west by the main line, on the east by a closely built-up area, on the north by the running shed and on the south by the Stores Dept. premises.

In addition to locomotive maintenance, repairs to wagons, carriages, cranes, and machinery in general were carried out as well as the large scale construction of new coaching stock.

Some relief was afforded when in 1925 the Bahía Blanca North Western workshops in Bahía Blanca were taken over, as these small workshops were quite well equipped to carry out repairs to all kinds of rolling stock.

The average number of workmen employed in the two workshops was about 3000 and 600 respectively.

It is not intended here to describe these workshops in detail, but the technically inclined reader may be referred to papers by the present author and F. Eastwood, published in the *Journal of the Institution of Locomotive Engineers* in Sept-Oct 1941 and Nov-Dec 1946 respectively.

As far as locomotive heavy repairs were concerned these workshops had to cope with the volume required to keep the fleet of steam locomotives in serviceable condition.

From 1928 to 1945 the numbers of steam locomotives on the books including BBNW Ry stock varied in accordance with the list shown on the following page.

Year	Number of Locomotives	Total locomotive kilometres run during the year
1928	794	33 166 167
1929	859	28 714 616
1930	857	32 859 698
1931	888	34 241 866
1932	907	30 366 410
1933	891	32 413 413
1934	873	30 569 366
1935	855	28 120 850
1936	844	35 290 105
1937	838	32 447 173
1938	838	34 928 990
1939	851	34 153 485
1940	850	33 760 364
1941	850	32 763 937
1942	844	29 924 157
1943	842	27 056 324
1944	839	23 747 048
1945	838	28 974 459

The heavy purchases up to 1932 are clearly evident, after which there were few additions except for the small pre-war purchases of 1938/39.

In the third column the effects of good or bad harvests can be seen as well as the decline during the war years, by which time competition from road transport was assuming serious proportions.

Taking an average of 850 locomotives and 33 million kilometres the annual average of 39 000 km per year may seem at first glance to be very low, but this by itself is a highly misleading figure as due to the large amount of seasonal traffic referred to in Chapter 2 many locomotives only worked intensively during a few months of the year.

On the other hand many main line passenger engines and most suburban tank engines averaged 100 000 km or over per year.

The shopping of locomotives for general repairs was subject to strict government control under somewhat archaic regulations drawn up before the beginning of the present century. The basis was the condition of the boiler and the rules called for a general repair with a hydraulic test of the boiler after 100 000 km had been run or three years had elapsed since the last general repair. In practice quite a proportion of the small wheeled freight engines were in need of a general repair by the time they reached the 100 000 km mark, and some were really due before that, but on the other hand there were many other engines which could easily have been allowed to run well over the arbitrary figure and still be in good shape. With a little more flexibility in the regulations the average kilometres run could easily have been increased and the load on the workshops reduced in proportion.

After some years, happily, it became possible to obtain 'extensions' of up to 20 000 km for certain engines, subject to their passing a test in steam by a government inspector.

In order to attain the annual kilometres run it was necessary to carry out 18 to 22 general repairs per month at Escalada and 4 to 5 general repairs per month at Bahía Blanca. A close liaison was always maintained with the Running Department in order to plan the monthly programmes well in advance and to reconcile the traffic requirements with the workshops capacity. It was necessary to maintain as far as possible a judicious mixture of tank engines, tender engines, two cylinder engines, three cylinder engines, etc, and due to the seasonal nature of many services the time of year had its influence also. On the whole the system worked very well and it was seldom that an engine had to be withdrawn from traffic before the date on which it was programmed to enter shops.

The government control was exercised by a body known as the 'National Railway Direction' which maintained a group of qualified engineers who had the job of inspecting every locomotive, carriage, and wagon prior to its return to service after general repair. They also witnessed the hydraulic tests on boilers under repair or when presented for extensions of certificates, and supervised the examinations of drivers and firemen.

Generally speaking everything in this connection usually ran quite smoothly and any minor differences of opinion which did arise were quickly ironed out.

The tendency for adhering to the strict letter of the law was occasionally a bone of contention, and in this connection the limit of absurdity was reached when the railways began to import locomotives completely assembled and ready for the road instead of dismantled and having to be re-erected on site. When new boilers were received dismantled there was never any fuss made about letting the inspectors see them under hydraulic test, although it was considered to be an unnecessary refinement from the technical point of view, but when they demanded that assembled locomotives should be stripped to enable a hydraulic test to be made, it was quite another matter and a definite issue was made of this. Fortunately the engineer in charge of the 'Direction' at that time was a man with plenty of common sense so the works certificates of hydraulic tests made in Britain were accepted by the national authorities.

One of the many curious things which happened after nationalization took place in 1948 was that the government inspectors simply disappeared without warning or advice. In spite of this all inspections were carried out meticulously by the workshops staff and certificates signed by the respective works managers were filed against the day when the inspectors would return. For as long as the writer remained in the service, that is, until the middle of 1951, no inspectors were seen, so advantage was taken of this to allow the average kilometres before general repair to increase slightly, in practice to about 115 000 km or 15 per cent increase. Far from having any detrimental effect on maintenance this measure actually tended to improve matters as hitherto there had always been something of a tendency to skip maintenance on engines which on a kilometrage basis were shortly due to enter shops. With the knowledge that the former top limit would no longer be applied strictly and that any engine might be required to exceed it substantially according to circumstances, more care was taken and fewer failures in service were recorded as a result.

Before concluding this chapter it may be of interest to add a few details concerning the main workshops and the running sheds, which also played their part in locomotive maintenance.

REMEDIOS DE ESCALADA WORKSHOPS

As mentioned earlier these workshops, though considered to be of ample capacity at the time of their opening in 1901, began to have difficulty in coping with requirements during the period of World War I, and as time went on their lack of capacity became more and more evident.

For geographical reasons, as already pointed out, the possibilities of expansion were very restricted so gradually some of the open areas were reduced by the construction of additional buildings, which in turn tended to complicate the freedom of movement so necessary in all railway workshops.

Round about 1930 the system of double shift working had to be introduced and eventually this was extended to cover practically the whole of the main and automatic machine shops, the carriage and wagon machine shop, the forging machines in the smithy, and part of the sawmill. This system has a number of drawbacks as regards adequate supervision etc, but there was no alternative; not only was there no money available to purchase additional machine tools, but there was virtually no place to put them if they had been purchased.

Fortunately the wisdom and foresight of Mr Saccaggio and his advisers of earlier years had caused him to equip the workshops as efficiently as possible prior to the advent of the critical period.

The main machine shop equipment included the latest models of centre lathes, vertical boring lathes, wheel lathes, milling, shaping, grinding, and drilling machines. The automatic machine shop had a fine array of modern capstan and turret lathes, while the toolroom and diesel shops each had their quota of the most modern machine tools to cater for their specialized requirements.

In the smithy modern drop stamps and 'Ajax' forging machines were outstanding aids to quantity production, as were the air-operated jolt moulding machines in the foundry, as well as the latest woodworking machines and spray painting equipment on the carriage and wagon side. Welding, both by the oxy-acetylene and electric processes, was highly developed, and internal transport facilities were always maintained at an adequate level. Lifting facilities in all sections were good.

As the workshops were located in the proximity of the capital there was seldom much difficulty in obtaining labour.

The outbreak of World War II in 1939 presented a problem as a considerable proportion of the labour force was of Italian nationality, and also a sprinkling of Germans and Austrians. It was decided—wisely as it transpired—to do nothing about this situation at all. Most of the Germans and Austrians disappeared of their own accord, but the Italians remained and in time many of them became active supporters of the Allied Red Cross fund and other similar activities. There was not a single case of sabotage or similar unpleasantness.

The training of apprentices in the workshops had an awkward obstacle to face. All male Argentinians must undergo a period of one or two years' military service on reaching the age of twenty. This meant that boys entering at the minimum permissible age of sixteen would not complete a normal five years' apprenticeship without this inevitable interruption occurring. In addition employers are obliged to pay a proportion of their wages to all men while on military service and to hold their jobs open for their return, so as happened also in the running sheds the tendency was to keep the quota of apprentices as low as possible, which in many ways was a pity as competent boilermakers, coppersmiths, and blacksmiths, amongst others, became increasingly difficult to find.

In order to obtain the best results from the modern plant and equipment the wise procedure of engaging specialized British contract foremen for most sections was followed. While most of these had retired or left at the time of nationalization they had been there long enough to train competent Argentine nationals to succeed them.

The following list enumerates the different sections of the Escalada workshops with approximate average number of men required for maximum production in each case:

Locomotive Section	*Approximate number of men*
Erecting and Tender Shops	300
Main Machine Shop	250
Fitting Shop	60
Boiler Shop	250
Coppersmiths and Tube Shop	100
Brass Finishing Shop	60
Automatic Machine Shop	100
Forge and Blacksmiths Shop	200
Iron and Brass Foundries	200
Tool Room	50
Heavy Diesel Repair Shop	20
Diesel Railcar Repair Shop	50
Millwrights and General Shop	100
Total	1740

Carriage and Wagon Section	
Carriage Repair and New Carriage Construction Shops	350
Wagon and Lifting Shops	300
Frame Shop	60
Machine Shop	100
Paint Shop	200
Tinsmiths Shop	40
Nickel Plating Shop	20
Upholsterers Shop	60
Sawmill	150
Joiners Shop	50
Yard Gang	20
Total	1350
Grand Total	3090

BAHÍA BLANCA WORKSHOPS

These workshops which date from 1892 were the property of the Bahía Blanca and North Western Railway which was operated by the Buenos Aires and Pacific Railway until 1925.

The BAGS Ry inherited a compact, well designed, and practically self-contained organization which must have been a model of its kind when new.

The acquisition of these workshops enabled the load of locomotive repairs at Escalada to be relieved to some extent, but the former still had to maintain some 50 BBNW locomotives transferred at the same time. Most of the numerous shunting engines in the Bahía Blanca area were also attended to when necessary.

Carriage work was very limited, being confined to the few vehicles required for the Bahía Blanca suburban services. It was in the field of wagon repairs that these workshops provided the greatest assistance. Ample yard area was available and gradually adapted for wagon repairs. The dry climate of the zone did not prevent efficient working in the open, and the results of progressive belt working were most gratifying, it being easier to instal that method there than in the cramped facilities at Escalada.

The locomotive erecting shop with two 30 ton overhead cranes was quite adequate for the types of locomotives dealt with. For wagon work steam travelling cranes were employed. The small foundry and blacksmiths shops were also adequate. In the machine shop most of the machines were rather old but still capable of doing good work. A few more modern machines were provided as opportunities presented themselves. The increase in wagon repair work meant that wheel lathes and some other machines had to be put on double shift.

Works managers and their assistants were usually British contract staff who after nationalization were succeeded by some of the very competent Argentine shop foremen.

The normal complement of workmen was as follows:

Section	Approximate number of men
Erecting and Fitting Shop	80
Machine and brass shop	50
Boiler and copper Shop	50
Blacksmith's Shop	40
Foundry	60
Carriage repairs	30
Wagon repair work	200
Paint shop	20
Waste recuperation and soaking plant	30
General labour	20
Total	580

RUNNING SHEDS

The traction organization consisted of seven locomotive districts with headquarters at Remedios de Escalada, Tolosa (La Plata), Empalme Lobos, Mar del Plata, Tandil, Olavarría, and Ingeniero White (Bahía Blanca).

The two largest running sheds were those at Remedios de Escalada and Ingeniero White, each of which had an allocation of 150/200 engines, and all the remaining districts had their principal sheds at the respective headquarters, with quotas of 50/100 engines.

At kilometre 1 near the Constitucion terminus there was a round house of some fifteen stalls which served mainly as a turn-round garage for mainline passenger engines working in from other districts.

The Ingeniero White district had important secondary running sheds at Saavedra and Neuquén, the Tandil district had similar sub-sheds at Ayacucho and Tres Arroyos, others being Las Flores in the Olavarria district and Sevigne in the Mar del Plata district.

Most of the running sheds were of the straight-through type but those at Tolosa and Ingeniero White included small round houses.

In addition there were numerous small sheds or servicing points located as required for branch-line services, etc.

All principal sheds were equipped with drop pits or sheer legs but the equipment of machine tools was in most cases limited to a few general purpose machines. It was not the railway's policy to carry out extensive repairs in running sheds, but rather to concentrate this class of work in the main workshops and the objective was to carry out workshop overhauls in such a thorough manner that workshops' attention was reduced to a minimum between scheduled overhauls, as in fact was the case. Another factor was that it was uneconomical to provide wheel lathes and other special purpose machines at running sheds where they could only be in use very intermittently over long periods.

Obviously a very close liaison had to be maintained between the running sheds and the workshops and to that end special inspectors and chasers were located in the latter to attend to the requirements of the former.

Transport of materials between workshops and running sheds always received high priority and on the whole the system worked very well.

Most of the District Locomotive Superintendents and their principal assistants were engineers on contract from Britain, but as time went on it became possible to fill a number of such posts with highly experienced and competent Argentine personnel.

In the early years of the century many engine drivers were brought out on contract from Britain and from these it was possible to build up a corps of shed foremen and locomotive inspectors of very high standard. At the date of nationalization, however, very few of these most worthy men remained but their local replacements for the most part proved entirely capable of carrying on the same fine traditions which seem to come naturally to experienced railwaymen all over the world.

One tale of the old British drivers is perhaps worth mentioning. Shortly after nationalization the writer was asked one day to see a Mr James Reid who had called with a card of presentation from a friend. It was something of a shock when Mr Reid was ushered in to see an almost coal-black Andean Indian from one of the far Western provinces who did not understand a word of English.

He explained that his father had been an engine driver from Glasgow who had married a local girl and she accompanied him on leave after his first five years' service. Thus it came about that this visitor had been born in Glasgow and was therefore a British national, though he had sailed for Argentina within a month and had never returned to his native land.

As Spanish normally was spoken in his home he had never learned any English, but he had been quite well educated and had joined the Central Córdoba Railway as an apprentice coppersmith, becoming a qualified tradesman in due course.

When his railway was taken over by the State Railway in 1937 there was a general clearing out of foreign personnel and as Reid had omitted to take out naturalization papers he fell under the axe in spite of being to all intents and purposes 100 per cent Argentine. No such short-sighted restrictions were imposed with the general nationalization of 1948 and at that time competent coppersmiths, like competent boilermakers, were exceedingly hard to find, so there was no hesitation in engaging Reid on the spot and according to all reports he proved an excellent investment.

The problem of traction staff including footplate men was always rather a difficult one with numbers required fluctuating considerably on account of the seasonal traffic peaks already mentioned. In general it meant many temporary promotions with gaps in the lowest grades covered by whatever casual labour happened to be available. A heavy outlay in payments for overtime was also inevitable.

Manning of the more remote sheds was also a problem at times as union insistence on the rights of senior men to claim transfers to the larger centres often meant that staff with least experience had to be allocated to points where supervision was less comprehensive. Nevertheless many a first-class shed man was evolved through the hard experience of being left practically on his own and being obliged either to make good or get out.

Suitable housing, even in some of the larger centres, was a matter which also gave rise to a certain amount of trouble and was in fact one of the weaker aspects of the whole organization which at the time of writing is not yet properly solved, the same difficulties being applicable to the staffs of the Traffic and Way and Works Depts to a greater or lesser degree.

The training of apprentices in the sheds proved in practice to be an excellent thing and if it had been possible to develop this practice on a larger scale the results undoubtedly would have warranted the extra expenditure involved.

In spite of all the difficulties, however, running shed maintenance over most of the period under review was on the whole highly satisfactory.

6

Description and History of the Locomotives, Class by Class

CLASS 1—FIG. 1

These were 4-4-2 passenger tank engines with two outside cylinders 16 in × 24 in and coupled wheels 5 ft 8 in diameter.

In the year 1889 they were converted from 4-4-0 tender engines class 6 of typical Beyer Peacock lineage, original building date 1883.

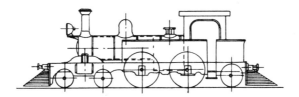

Fig. 1 Class 1 Passenger tank 184-195

In 1924 nine of the original class Nos. 184 to 195 were still in service performing useful work on the frequent, but lightly loaded suburban and branch line trains in the Bahía Blanca are shown on sketch map C. They continued mainly on these services until 1929, when they were withdrawn and replaced by class 1B.

CLASS 1B—FIG. 2

These were 4-4-4 passenger tank engines with coupled wheels no less than 6 ft 0 in diameter, which was a high figure for tank engines in Argentina.

They were originally built by Beyer Peacock for the BA Western Railway, between 1903 and 1906 and became redundant when the suburban lines of that railway were electrified.

In 1929 eight, numbered between 174 and 183 were purchased by the BA Great Southern to replace the smaller class 1 engines which had reached the end of their useful life; a ninth engine, No. 143, was likewise purchased in 1936.

Normally this class had cylinders 18 in × 24 in but Nos. 175, 176, and 177 had cylinders 17 in × 26 in.

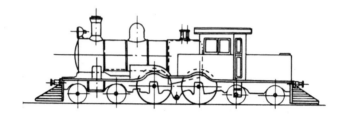

Fig. 2 Class 1B Passenger tank 143 and 174-183

They were spirited performers on light branch trains and very popular with their crews, but unlike most similar classes were never converted to burn oil.

They were still in service at the time of the nationalization of 1948, but had all been scrapped by 1967.

CLASS 3C—FIG. 3

This class consisted of ten outside cylinder 0-4-0 tank engines, Nos. 2031 to 2040.

Nos. 2031 to 2035 were built by Kitsons in 1902, and Nos. 2036 to 2040 by R. Stephensons in 1906.

With cylinders 14 in × 21 in, coupled wheels 3 ft 2 in diameter and a weight in working order of only $26\frac{1}{4}$ tons they could literally go into every hole and corner on the system.

They were fitted with Kitsons patent outside valve gear which was applied to many other similar engines manufactured by that Company, such as those for the Hull and Barnsley Railway in England, which were practically identical except for the gauge.

Water was carried in a well tank between the frames, the apparent side tank plates being merely a protection for the motion.

Apart from operating on a number of the most precarious and lightly laid sidings throughout the line, they were to be found in several of the larger running sheds for moving 'dead' engines on and off the turntables and similar jobs.

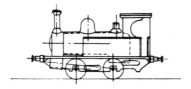

Fig. 3 Class 3C Shunting tank 2031–2040

In 1943 No. 2040 was sold to the Ministry of War and No. 2031 was sold to a large brewery, for work on their respective sidings, and as far as is known are still extant.

The remainder were all in service in 1948, but had disappeared by 1967.

CLASS 6B—FIG 4

Between 1897 and 1904, twenty-five class 6 4-4-0 tender engines Nos. 251 to 275 were converted from simple to compound to form class 6B.

As converted they had an HP cylinder 17 in diameter and an LP cylinder $24\frac{1}{2}$ in diameter with a common stroke of 24 in, with a boiler pressure of 175 lb/in^2.

Fig. 4 Class 6B 2 cyl. comp. Passenger 251–275

Like the class 1 conversions the coupled wheels were 5 ft 8 in diameter which became the standard size for mixed traffic engines on the railway right up to and including the class 15B of 1948.

Only six were left in 1924 and they did not survive many more years.

In their prime they did good work on outer suburban and light main-line trains, some of them figuring in the earliest trials of oil burning as far back as 1909.

This was the only case on record of a conversion from simple to compound, and before their final withdrawal the reverse process of conversion from compound to simple had already begun with other classes.

In general appearance the class 6B was a typical Beyer Peacock product of its time, very similar to others built for Spain, New South Wales, and elsewhere. The extended smokebox on the diagram was a later addition.

CLASS 7—FIG 5

This was a typical Beyer Peacock outside cylinder 2-6-0 tender engine. The original class of twenty-eight was built in 1885 at Gorton.

Some had cylinders 17 in × 24 in and others 18 in × 24 in.

The coupled wheels were 5 ft 2 in diameter and the working pressure 150 lb/in^2. Two engines were converted to burn oil in their later days.

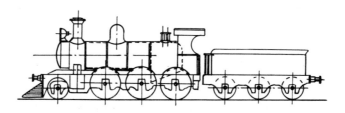

Fig. 5 Class 7 Mixed traffic 3001-3028

Extended smokeboxes were provided, probably on account of the use of wood fuel, which were unusual in that the extension had a diameter the same as that of the smokebox door seating ring, smaller than that of the smokebox proper.

This rather unsightly feature was perpetuated on classes 7B and 8A, but after these, subsequent classes were provided with smokeboxes of more conventional appearance.

Until the advent in 1903 of the first 2-8-0 compounds, class 11, the class 7 engines had a considerable share in the rapidly growing goods traffic and must have been very hard pressed at times.

By 1924 only Nos. 3013, 3016, 3025, and 3026 survived and two or three years later they had all been withdrawn.

Class 7A was a compound version of class 7, but had all been withdrawn by 1924.

CLASS 7B—FIG. 6

These twenty-eight two-cylinder compound 2-6-0 mixed traffic engines Nos. 3071 to 3098 were built by Beyer Peacock & Co. in 1901.

The last batch, Nos. 3081 to 3098 had large cabs with side windows which from then on became the standard for all tender engines.

The HP cylinder was 18 in diameter and the LP 26 in diameter, the stroke being 26 in.

Coupled wheels were the standard mixed traffic size of 5 ft 8 in.

For their first few years they bore the brunt of the heaviest main line services all over the system until the advent of the larger classes 11 and 12 from 1903 onwards.

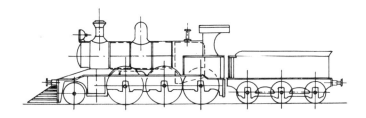

Fig. 6 Class 7B Comp. Mixed traffic 3071–3098

Thereafter they were relegated progressively to less important branch duties and in the late nineteen-thirties when compounding had definitely gone out of favour they were laid aside as and when heavy boiler repairs became necessary.

Thus they remained in cold storage, as it were, with one or two exceptions which worked on the branches south of La Plata.

In 1949, however, the acute shortage of motive power prior to the advent of the first regular diesel orders prompted a re-examination of their possibilities.

Several were found to have boilers in reasonably good condition so as a first step two were repaired and converted to burn oil.

They proved so successful that two much more useful class 7D engines were released for heavier duties.

Two others with good boilers had broken LP cylinders and no pattern for these remained in existence.

A spare flat-valve cylinder for class 8A was found, however, that could be adapted, so this was fitted on the LP side of No. 3086, which was thus converted to simple after the necessary modifications to the steam and exhaust pipes, etc. Oil burning equipment was also fitted.

In the case of the second engine, No. 3071, no similar spare cylinder could be found, so the problem was solved by fitting a cast-iron bush 18 in inside diameter inside the existing LP cylinder, and with other similar alterations, as in the case of No 3086, a second most useful simple 2–6–0 with a tractive effort of 17 350 lb was produced.

These two engines were tried out successfully on the passenger services over the 372 km branch line from Bahía Blanca to Toay, making two badly needed class 11B engines available for main line goods work.

The measures taken with these class 7B engines, together with other steps taken about the same time with classes 8A, 11, 11A, 12, and 12A to be detailed under their respective headings, were good examples of how sturdy British products around 50 years old, with negligible outlay above the cost of a normal overhaul, could be modified to produce a quite substantial increase in the available motive power as a whole.

The class 7B survivors, however, had succumbed to the diesel age and had been scrapped by 1967.

No. 3096 of this class had the distinction in 1921 of heading the first train to reach Patagones, and to mark the occasion received the name 'Maragata'.

CLASS 7D—FIG. 7

This class of 2–6–0 mixed traffic tender engines originated with No. 3101 built by Beyer Peacock in 1912 as a two-cylinder compound, class 7C.

A further twenty-one, Nos. 3102 to 3122, were delivered from the same builders in 1912/14, these being two-cylinder superheater oil burning simples with cylinders 19 in × 26 in and coupled wheels 5 ft 8 in diameter.

In 1926 No. 3101 was converted to simple and incorporated into class 7D.

The original boiler pressure was 150 lb/in^2, but this was later increased to 175 lb/in^2.

This was one of the most useful and versatile classes the railway ever possessed, being equally successful on light passenger branch trains, goods trains on secondary lines and livestock trains throughout the system.

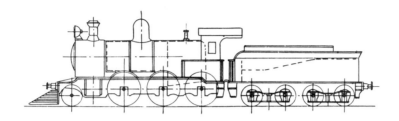

Fig. 7 Class 7D Mixed traffic 3101–3122

They were easy to maintain, and economical on oil fuel.

This was the first class, apart from the four-cylinder Vulcan compounds of 1906 class 12B to be fitted with Walschaerts valve gear, which from then on became standard.

In 1967 the class of twenty-two engines was still intact.

CLASS 8—Fig. 8

This class of eighteen outside-cylinder 2–6–2 side-tank engines, Nos. 3301 to 3318, was produced by fitting boilers and cylinders from the ubiquitous class 6 already mentioned on new frames. The conversions took place between 1898 and 1903.

The cylinders were 16 in × 24 in and the coupled wheels were 4 ft $7\frac{1}{2}$ in which later became the railway's standard size for goods engines.

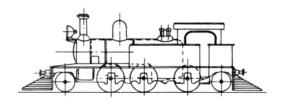

Fig. 8 Class 8 Shunting tank 3301–3318

The class 8 engines were never fitted for oil burning and spent most of their later years on light duties around Bahía Blanca.

By 1924 only six were left and these all disappeared a few years later.

CLASS 8A—FIG. 9

Unlike most of the earliest classes which were predominately Beyer Peacock, this class of outside cylinder 2-6-2 tank engines came from the North British Locomotive Co.

Nos. 3321 to 3342 were built in 1906 and Nos. 3343 to 3354 in 1907 making a total of thirty-four engines.

Using saturated steam as originally built the cylinders were 18 in × 26 in with slide valves. As time went on most of the class were superheated and fitted with cylinders 19 in × 26 in and piston valves. Latterly all were equipped for burning oil.

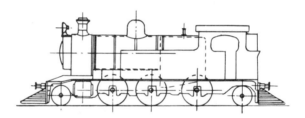

Fig. 9 Class 8A Mixed traffic tank 3321-3354

The coupled wheels were 5 ft 2 in diameter which was an unusual size for the Southern Railway.

The boiler was of large proportions for the period, with a barrel 5 ft $4\frac{1}{2}$ in diameter by 11 ft 1 in long, 1660 square feet of heating surface when saturated, and 27 square feet of grate area, the working pressure being 160 lb/in^2.

A story used to be current that these engines were designed and built for a railway in India and diverted to Argentina, but it has been impossible to trace any official record of this. Whatever the truth may be, the fact is that the class 8A engines were a remarkably good investment for the railway, being real maids of all work and able to perform efficiently every possible job within their rather limited fuel and water capacity.

Their $16\frac{1}{2}$ ton maximum axle loading gave them a very wide range of availability.

By the end of 1924 only twenty-seven of the larger 2-6-4 class 8E engines had entered service so at that date and for some years subsequently the class 8A still played a considerable part in the intense Buenos Aires suburban services, for which they were originally intended. Later they gravitated to branch line and shunting services and were always much in evidence in the port area at Bahía Blanca.

Much later, in 1949, after nationalization, when a temporary crisis arose on the Buenos Aires suburban services due to some minor troubles with the class 8E, it was decided to press some of the old 8A's into passenger service once again. After a good overhaul and being fitted with the latest type of vacuum ejector, the half-dozen veterans so treated responded nobly and successfully filled the gap until the situation of the 8E's returned to normal.

As late as mid-1967 at least one class 8A could be seen as station pilot at the Plaza Constitución terminus, while others were in evidence in the marshalling yard at Kilometre 5, apparently good for a few more years.

As far as can be ascertained no spare boilers class 8A were ever purchased, so their condition after 60 years of active service is an outstanding testimonial to the quality of the products of the British manufacturers in the early days of the twentieth century.

CLASS 8B—FIG. 10

These ten powerful 2-6-2 outside cylinder tank engines, Nos. 3401 to 3410 were built in 1908 by Naysmith Wilson & Co.

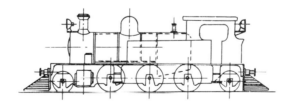

Fig. 10 Class 8B Shunting tank 3401-3410

They had cylinders 17 in × 24 in, coupled wheels 4 ft 4 in diameter and a tractive effort of 19 200 lb at 85 per cent boiler pressure of 180 lb/in^2.

The maximum axle loading was just over 15 tons, thus enabling them to be used on light branches and sidings.

As mentioned earlier the whole of the Province of Buenos Aires is a vast alluvial plain with only very few places where stone or rock can be found. One of these is the area around Azul and Tandil in the Sierras Bayas hills. With the railway's own need for stone for track ballast, plus the demand for building, road-making etc, it is not surprising that from early days many stone quarries were developed wherever possible. In this respect the Sierras Bayas area is particularly prolific, with many short connecting lines and quarry sidings.

The class 8B engines were ordered specifically for this class of service, on which they were eminently successful, so much so that most were still on their original jobs after 59 years, based on the running sheds at Azul, Hinojo, and Tandil.

In May 1967 No. 3408 was observed in a fresh coat of paint on a trial run after overhaul in the Escalada workshops.

None of the class were ever superheated, but three engines were converted to burn oil.

CLASS 8C—FIG. 11

This class was a tank engine version of the 2–6–0 mixed traffic engines class 7D with the addition of a trailing pony truck.

They had the same cylinders and boiler, the same 5 ft 8 in diameter coupled wheels and were superheated when built. They were in due course all converted to burn oil.

Nos. 3451 to 3460 came from R. Stephenson & Sons in 1913, and Nos. 3461 to 3491 from the North British Locomotive Co. in 1914, a total of forty-one in all.

They at once took over the bulk of the Buenos Aires suburban services including the longer runs unsuitable for the class 8A due to the restricted fuel capacity of the latter.

The class 8C bore the brunt of this heavy and rapidly growing traffic for over twenty years, until the class 8E began to appear, by which time trains of ten large coaches with an empty weight of over 400 tons were not uncommon. The unmerciful thrashing they received during this period undoubtedly was the cause of troubles with loose cylinders and other structural weaknesses which developed in later years and which contributed to the withdrawal of most of the class after nationalization.

They had a remarkable turn of speed and in their heyday were extremely economical to operate and to maintain.

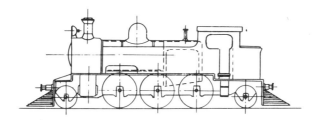

Fig. 11 Class 8C Passenger tank 3451–3491

After the arrival of the 8E's they took over the lighter suburban trains originating at Temperley and La Plata until 1938 when a large purchase of Drewry railcars displaced them.

Some thereafter worked in the Bahía Blanca and Tandil districts and all were still in service in 1948 at the time of the take-over.

By 1967 only three of the class had survived.

CLASS 8D—FIG. 12

The forty 2-6-2 tank engines class 8D were the standard for heavy shunting from their arrival until the present day.

The first ten, Nos. 3501 to 3510 were built by Beyer Peacock in 1913. As originally delivered they were non-superheater and coal burning, but in due course were superheated and equipped for oil burning.

Subsequently, thirty additional engines were delivered, Nos. 3150 to 3164 by Beyer Peacock and Nos. 3165 to 3179 by the North British Locomotive Co., both lots in 1926.

These later engines were superheated and equipped for oil burning when built. The 19 in × 26 in cylinders were the same as for classes 7D, 8C, and 11B, the boilers were duplicate with those of classes 7D and 8C and the 4 ft $7\frac{1}{2}$ in diameter coupled wheels were the same as on classes 11, 11A, and 11B.

About three quarters of the class spent the whole of their life in the shunting yards around Buenos Aires, mostly in the principal marshalling yard at Kilometre 5, and also in the terminals at Solá, Casa Amarilla, and Ingeniero Brian, the situation of which calls for a large volume of transfer work. Others of the class took part in the heavy shunting in the Bahía Blanca port area and a few other places.

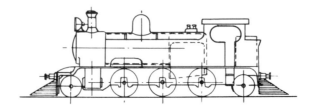

Fig. 12 Class 8D Shunting tank 3150–3179 & 3501–3510

When towards the end of World War II the question of diesel shunters for post-war developments was under study, it was felt that as regards availability the diesel could not improve on that of the oil burning class 8D.

The engines habitually left Escalada shed for Kilometre 5 on Sunday nights and did not return until the following Saturday night. They remained in steam during the whole period, only gathering at a central fuel and watering point in the yard at predetermined times. There would normally be one fitter on duty there, but as a rule he had a very easy time.

This standard of performance had so far been sufficient to prevent or at least postpone indefinitely the purchase of diesel shunters, and at mid 1967 the whole class 8D was still hard at work as usual.

CLASS 8E—FIG. 13

This class was the ultimate development of a suburban tank engine on the Southern Railway, weighing no less than 101 tons in working order.

They were the first three-cylinder simple engines to be acquired, and apart from the nine Vulcan 4–6–0 four-cylinder compounds class 12B of 1907 were the first on the railway to have crank axles.

Prior to their appearance crank axles on the 5 ft 6 in gauge had been very rare throughout the world.

Sixty-one class 8E 2–6–4 tank engines were built. Nos. 3530 to 3541 were built by Hawthorn Leslie in 1923–24, Nos. 3542 to 3556 by the North British Locomotive Co. in 1924–25, Nos. 3557 to 3581 by Vulcan Foundry in 1926–27, and Nos. 3582 to 3591 also by Vulcan in 1930.

The three cylinders were $17\frac{1}{2}$ in × 26 in and the coupled wheels 5 ft 8 in diameter. Three independent sets of Walschaerts valve motion were employed.

The 5 ft $4\frac{1}{2}$ in diameter boiler was duplicate with that already in service in the class 12A and 12D 4–6–0 tender engines. The working pressure was 200 lb/in². All were superheated and equipped for burning oil when built.

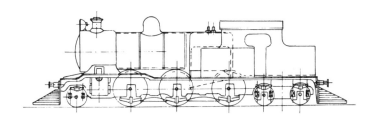

Fig. 13 Class 8E 3 cyl. Passenger tank 3530–3591

Other original fittings included Weir feed pumps and feed water heaters and mechanical lubricators, but in accordance with the ruling policy these and most gadgets of a similar nature were later dispensed with as it was considered that the cost of their maintenance outweighed any advantages gained in the form of lower fuel consumption, etc.

The class 8E quickly became masters of the enormous suburban traffic around Buenos Aires. The number of passengers carried annually had risen from $22\frac{1}{2}$ millions in 1913 to $43\frac{1}{2}$ millions in 1925, and for years thereafter continued to increase. For some years, however, they were barred from the direct line to La Plata via Quilmes, due to civil engineering restrictions on the Sarandí viaduct, which line continued to be worked mainly by the lighter class 8C whose maximum axle load was $16\frac{1}{2}$ tons compared with nearly 19 tons for class 8E. By the time the last 8E's were ordered these restrictions had been removed, and the class became the standard over the whole of the suburban network.

Their history over the next twenty years is one of hard slogging, together with high averages of 10 000 km or more per month and an exceptionally low fuel consumption.

It is true that they required efficient maintenance and for the most part this was provided, but they were extremely reliable on the whole and must have proved an excellent investment.

In 1959 or thereabouts most of a series of 1900 h.p. Alsthom diesels were demoted from their original main-line work to suburban services which released some 8E's and finally in 1962 a batch of forty-five American diesels of 1300 h.p. arrived. They were a typical 'off the shelf' job having standard gauge bodies on broad gauge bogies, and being considerably lower and narrower than the coaches they haul, give the trains a curious look.

On the assumption that the 8E's were finished a considerable number were broken up, but fortunately for the railway twenty-one were spared and kept in working order.

When in 1966 diesel availability reached a low ebb, several diagrams had 8E's again assigned to them, a situation which persisted in mid 1967. Several others were then engaged on empty coach duties in and out the terminus, so even after 44 years of heavy service some of the class were still to be seen and admired in their old haunts, and the prospects of their remaining in harness indefinitely were strong.

Towards the end of 1967, in fact, the diesel situation had deteriorated to such an extent that no less than fifteen class 8E locomotives were incorporated into the normal suburban train diagrams and very soon were performing with every satisfaction. They were nicely painted and lined out as in the early days and looked and sounded as good as ever.

One episode in which the 8E's played a part is worth recording. After nationalization, the new authorities were full of ideas particularly in the direction of making innovations and changes. In 1949 the word went out that the locomotives must be painted in brighter colours instead of the standard black with yellow lining.

It was pointed out that with the acute shortage of cleaning staff then available, the brighter colours, apart from their being more expensive, would quickly lose all the intended effect through lack of cleaning.

In spite of this the idea was insisted upon and the Mechanical Dept. of the Southern (by then the General Roca Railway) was asked to submit several local tank engines in different colours from which the choice of the new standard colour would be made.

The 8E's of course were the obvious choice; one was painted in Caledonian blue, one in North British olive green, one in Midland red, and one in North Eastern green and they all looked very handsome indeed.

The North British olive green won the day, to the great satisfaction of the writer as a former NBR man, and for some time this colour was applied to all the principal classes as they passed through shops.

The inevitable happened, of course, and after a few months in service the new colour was seldom distinguishable from the original black so in the best face-saving tradition stocks of the new colour were allowed to run out without provision for renewal and thus as in numerous other cases of a similar nature, the matter died a natural death.

CLASS 9—FIG. 14

This class consisted of eleven small outside cylinder tank engines Nos. 351 to 361 built by Beyer Peacock in 1898.

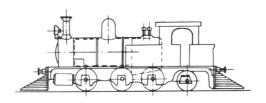

Fig. 14 Class 9 Shunting tank 351–361

They had cylinders 16 in × 22 in, coupled wheels 3 ft 8 in diameter, and a working pressure of 150 lb/in^2. With an axle load of only 13 tons they were very handy for working in port and industrial sidings on which service they lasted for many years. By 1948 two had been withdrawn and the remainder disappeared shortly after.

CLASS 11—FIG. 15

These 2-8-0 two-cylinder compounds were first introduced in 1903 and were the forerunners of many similar Von Borries compound goods engines not only on the Southern, but also on the Western and Central Argentine Railways, all being practically identical except for some details.

One of the most familiar sights on the Argentine pampas for many years was one of these compounds ambling along with a goods or cattle train, and judging from the mild tone of the exhaust, making light of it.

Undoubtedly during the earlier years of rapid development of the railways, this type of locomotive was very useful and economical on the mostly level main lines, but as time went on increased loads together with the need for greater speeds and better acceleration on single lines, the capacity of which was nearing saturation point at certain times of the year, brought about the gradual switch-over to single expansion.

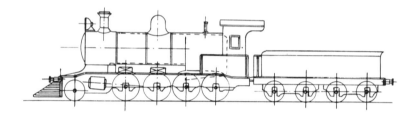

Fig. 15 Class 11 2 cyl. Comp. goods 4001–4040

This was more so on the Southern as the other two railways mentioned persevered with compounds in one form or another until the end of their separate existence.

The first batch of class 11, Nos. 4001 to 4015, were built by Beyer Peacock in 1903. These had the springs for the first and second pairs of coupled wheels placed above the axleboxes and the cylinders drove on the second coupled axle.

Subsequent additions were as follows:

Nos. 4016 to 4040, built by the Vulcan Foundry in 1907, making a total of forty for the class. This later batch had underhung springs for all coupled wheels and the cylinders drove on the third coupled axle.

All had an HP cylinder 19 in diameter and an LP cylinder $27\frac{1}{2}$ in diameter with a stroke of 26 in and the coupled wheels were 4 ft $7\frac{1}{2}$ in diameter.

The working pressure of 200 lb/in^2 was on the high side for the period and the maximum axle load of $12\frac{1}{2}$ tons ensured route availability all over the system.

From about 1923 the whole of the class except Nos. 4014 and 4023 were fitted with superheaters.

They were widely dispersed throughout the line and as compounds were never equipped to burn oil, many being based on small sheds where oil fuelling facilities did not exist.

They were still on the books in 1948, but except for the four converted to simple, class 11S, the class was extinct by mid 1967.

CLASS 11A—FIG. 16

These two-cylinder compound 2–8–0 goods engines Nos. 4041 to 4070 were built by the Vulcan Foundry in 1907–08, a total of thirty.

Instead of the Von Borries automatic intercepting valve in the smokebox, they had an intercepting valve above the HP cylinder, operated by the reversing lever, an arrangement which enabled greater effort to be applied when starting a train from rest.

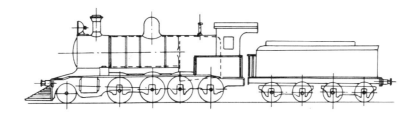

Fig. 16 Class 11A 2 cyl. Comp. goods 4041-4070

In all other respects they were identical to the later engines of class 11, and most of what has been written about that class applies equally well to class 11A.

All were superheated in due course, with a new HP cylinder with piston valves instead of slide valves, also new smokebox and firebox tubeplates. The entire firebox was only renewed when its general condition called for this.

Like class 11 they burned coal or wood throughout their life as compounds.

Twenty-eight were in service in 1948, after which date fourteen were converted to simple, class 11S and by 1967 none of the compounds remained, though the simples were all still hard at work.

CLASS 11B—FIG. 17

This was in effect a two-cylinder simple version of classes 11 and 11A with the same boiler, wheels, wheel spacing, and axle loading.

No less than 100 were built altogether, as follows:

Nos. 4101 to 4120 by Beyer Peacock in 1914
Nos. 4121 to 4150 by German builders in 1914
Nos. 4151 to 4160 by the North British Locomotive Co. in 1915
Nos. 4161 to 4200 by the Vulcan Foundry in 1931–32.

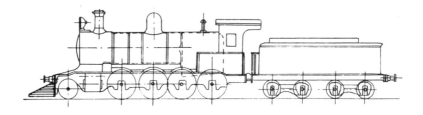

Fig. 17 Class 11B 2 cyl. goods 4101–4200

The cylinders 19 in × 26 in with piston valves and Walschaerts valve gear were the same as for classes 7D (2-6-0), 8C (2-6-2T), and 8D (2-6-2T). All were super-heated when built. Many were at one time or another equipped for burning oil.

These were the true maids-of-all-work in every corner of the system on goods trains, cattle trains, and certain shunting jobs. Several were used on branch line passenger trains and in this respect they monopolized the services on the very lightly constructed line from Bahía Blanca to Toay on the Bahía Blanca North Western system for many years. Prior to the 8E's being allowed to work over the Sarandi viaduct, the class 11B was occasionally employed on passenger trains between Buenos Aires and La Plata, as well as on branches radiating from the latter city.

In 1967 the class was intact save for No. 4147 which many years earlier was destroyed in an accident.

In 1965 a contract was given to a private company in Buenos Aires, called ASTARSA to give the class 11B very heavy overhauls as it was decided to keep them going indefinitely. This company turns out a good job, having well equipped workshops, and having the services of several very capable engineers formerly with the railways in France. Apart from normal general repair work new cabs and tender tanks were fitted, the sandboxes were placed on top of the boiler and a modified oil fuel control system fitted.

The earlier engines thus renovated after over 50 years of service appear to be capable of many more years of useful work.

CLASS 11C—FIG. 18

This was one of the heaviest and most powerful goods engines ever built for Argentina.

The 4–8–0 wheel arrangement with three cylinders and three sets of Walschaerts valve motion was adopted, this being the second three-cylinder class on the Southern Railway.

The first twenty-five, Nos. 4201 to 4225 were built by Armstrong Whitworth in 1924–25. No. 4203 was on exhibition at Wembley in the British Empire Exhibition of 1924, where she was greatly admired and with every justification. For many years she carried special plates on the cab sides to commemorate that event.

Although the engine alone weighed 84 tons in working order, the maximum axle load was just over 16 tons, thereby ensuring very good route availability.

In due course fifty more of these engines were built, Nos. 4226 to 4255 by Armstrong Whitworth, and Nos. 4256 to 4275 by Beyer Peacock, all in 1929.

In 1931 the latter batch, for accountancy reasons, had their numbers altered to 4280 and 4299 and figured on the books of the Bahía Blanca North Western Railway, but were by no means restricted to operate on that line. The later fifty engines had larger tenders and improved cabs. The whole class was superheated and equipped for oil burning when built.

The three cylinders were $17\frac{1}{2}$ in × 26 in coupled wheels 4 ft $7\frac{1}{2}$ in diameter, and the working pressure was 200 lb/in^2.

The first batch of twenty-five and fifteen of the second batch were fitted with Weir pumps and feed water heaters, but in accordance with later policy as mentioned in connection with class 8E, these fittings were subsequently eliminated.

With the coming of class 11C, the era of trains of 1500–2000 tons arrived, and they proved equal to dealing with trains as long as could be conveniently accommodated in certain passing loops, to say nothing of the increased loads imposed on the existing form of drawgear and couplings which at times caused rather a lot of breakages.

In terms of cargo handled and revenue earned this class must have paid for itself hands down within a comparatively short period.

As in most three cylinder designs maintenance was a little heavy, though no trouble was experienced with the crank axles, but in Argentina any inside motion is considered awkward and inaccessible by the staff and its attention could at times be improved.

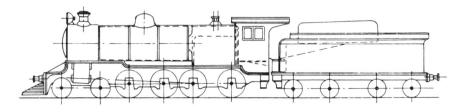

Fig. 18 Class 11C 3 cyl. heavy goods 4201–4275

Quite high running speeds were often attained and with such small coupled wheels wear and tear on the axleboxes was heavy. At one time a very heavy sleeping car train was run from Buenos Aires to the seaside resort of Mar del Plata, 400 km distant, every Friday throughout the holiday months and sometimes more frequently, with a return service on Sunday nights. This train which sometimes consisted of up to twenty heavy sleeping cars and a luggage van left Plaza Constitución at 10.30 p.m. but as there was no point in arriving too early at Mar del Plata the following morning, the schedule was a very easy one which synchronized quite well with and did not upset the nocturnal goods traffic. After various classes of engines had been tried out, it was found that a class 11C in good trim was ideal for this job, this being an example of their general utility and versatility.

As mentioned under class 11B, there is a private company called ASTARSA in Buenos Aires, which is well equipped for undertaking locomotive work. In 1957 the class 11C began to go through the ASTARSA shops when in need of heavy repairs and an excellent job has been made of the lot.

Modifications carried out include the fitting of Franklin automatic self-adjusting wedges for the coupled axleboxes which have given excellent results, in fact the engines so fitted run like sewing machines when in good trim. Improved exhaust pipes were applied with improved steaming as a result, and the sand boxes were placed on top of the boiler.

A new form of oil fuel equipment with independent controls, however, while

Class 6 4–4–0 No. 46, built 1883.
From this class Classes 1, 6B, and 8 were evolved

Class 8A No. 3346, taken at Llavalloll, February 1971

No. 4080 of Class 11S.
This class was converted from Classes 11 and 11A of 1903–1907

Class 12 compound

Mar del Plata afternoon express taking water at Grandara, 30 January 1909.
Locomotive No. 555 (old numbering),
Class 12A two-cylinder compound as originally built

Four-cylinder compound No. 3899, Class 12B

Four-cylinder compound Class 12B
on Mar del Plata express, January 1908

No. 3856 of Class 12F, converted from compound Class 12 of 1906

Class 12P No. 3210 at Circunvalacion station in January 1970

No. 3175, Class 8D, at Temperley 1968

Class 11B 2–8–0 No. 4144 as built.
Photographed at Carmen de Patagones, January 1971

Class 12D No. 3952, *Tordo*, at Remedios de Escalada, March 1971

Class 8E No. 3557 at Temperley, September 1970

Class 8E with Weir pump and heater,
also oil headlamps, as originally built

Class 11C No. 4203 at Wembley Exhibition in 1924

Class 11C 4-8-0 No. 4235 as modified by ASTARSA, 1960/61

Three-cylinder 2–8–0 No. 4314, Class 11D

Class 12E as originally built
with Weir pump and feed water heater

Class 12E No. 3922, *General Güemes*, fitted with exhaust steam injector and air brake for working train of 'Budd' cars, 1952. Photographed at Temperley, 1968

Class 12E No. 3926 *Brandsen* at Vela, October 1971

Garratt Class 14 No. 4859

Class 12H No. 3902 *Larrea* as built

Class 12H No. 3901 *Avellaneda* at Temperley 1968

Class 12G No. 3884 *Ciervo* of 1938.
Class 12 boiler of 1906 on new chassis

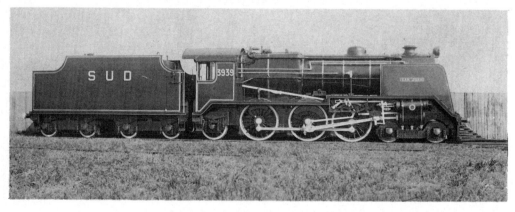

No. 3939 *San Juan*, Class 12K, when new

Class 12L No. 3003 *Lago Mascardi*, with Caprotti valve gear

Locomotive No. 2, Class BA Bahía Blanca North Western Railway
fitted with boiler ex Class 12B BAGS Railway

Class 75B No. 4 at Cerro Mesa, January 1971

Hunslett 4–6–0 tank engine, ex agricultural light railways,
at work in Corrientes, North Argentina, in 1960

Ex BA Pacific Railway (Bahía Blanca North Western Railway)
light 2–8–0 Class BB No. 460 as rebuilt
with second-hand Western Railway boiler

Class 75H No. 125 at El Maiten, January 1971

1700 h.p. diesel electric locomotive No. CM210

The first diesel electric mobile power house.
Two five-coach diesel electric trains coupled together
with mobile power houses UE1 and UE2 at the outer ends

probably in theory more efficient, does not always seem so in practice as the clouds of black smoke seem at times to bear witness, and it would seem that firemen of lesser experience find this apparatus more difficult to manipulate successfully than the standard combined apparatus to which reference is made on another page.

In spite of the advance of the diesel age, in mid 1967, the class 11C, still intact, continued to be the backbone of the heaviest goods and grain traffic on the Southern Railway, and they also take a share of the express services bringing in fruit from the Rio Negro valley over the final lap between Saavedra and Kilometre 5, a distance of nearly 600 km.

CLASS 11D—FIG. 19

This class consisted of thirty-five three-cylinder 2–8–0s intended as a light version of class 11C for working when necessary on some of the lighter branches. Their maximum axle load of 15 tons was one ton less than that of the latter class.

The entire class was built by Armstrong Whitworth in 1926-7. They were superheated and equipped for oil burning when built. The cylinders were $17\frac{1}{2}$ in × 26 in and the coupled wheels were 4 ft $7\frac{1}{2}$ in diameter as on class 11C. The

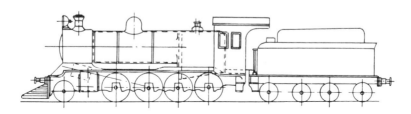

Fig. 19 Class 11D 3 cyl. heavy goods 4301-4335

boilers were of the same dimensions as those of the Vulcan four-cylinder compound 4–6–0s class 12B, the working pressure being 180 lb/in^2.

There is nothing very remarkable about the history of this class. Many were concentrated in the Tandil area where heavy stone and livestock traffic originates, and they had a reputation for doing excellent work on low fuel consumption.

When the Viedma to Bariloche line of the former State Railway was incorporated into the Southern system after nationalization, several 11D's were allocated to both passenger and goods services over the heavily graded section from Ingeniero Jacobacci to Bariloche, where they were most successful provided the standard of maintenance was kept up.

All were on the books in mid 1967, but they have not been modernized as in the case of classes 11B and 11C already mentioned, so unless there is a large-scale return to steam, which, however, seems not unlikely at the time of writing, their chances of survival for much longer are doubtful.

CLASS 11S—FIG. 20

When in March 1948 nationalization of the railways became an accomplished fact, the new authorities, in an endeavour to demonstrate how they could improve the services, set about altering timetables, accelerating services, programming additional trains, etc, the inevitable result being that the already precarious motive power situation was strained to its utmost limit.

Fortunately the Southern Railway received the thirty class 15B mixed traffic engines, in 1948-9, but for which the position would have been little short of disastrous. It must be remembered that since 1939, or over a period of nine years, not a single new steam locomotive had been placed in service.

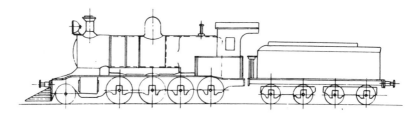

Fig. 20 Class 11S 2 cyl. simple goods 4080-4096

To those charged with the responsibility of operating these revised services, therefore, and in particular during the busy season, the task was not unlike trying to get a gallon and a half out of a one gallon tin, and one avenue which was explored was that of improving the performance of several existing classes of engines. Mention has been made of measures taken with classes 7B and 8A and in due course classes 12A, 12K, 15A, and 12P will be referred to. The class 11S was a direct outcome of this search for greater power. When the 2-8-0 compounds, classes 11 and 11A of 1903–08, were superheated, new HP cylinders with piston valves were fitted in place of the existing ones which had flat slide valves. By good fortune the castings for these new cylinders were symmetrical, that is to say they could be fitted equally well on either side of the engine. It was therefore decided to use one to convert a class 11A, to simple, as an experiment, modifying the steam and exhaust pipes, motion etc, accordingly.

This was duly carried out and the engine No. 4080 was a complete success, so much so that in due course the class was increased, to eighteen engines, four from class 11 and fourteen from class 11A.

The tractive effort was increased from 23 658 lb to 27 060 lb at 80 per cent boiler pressure, equal to almost 15 per cent, and the steaming was improved thanks to the modified blast arrangement. The converted engines were thus enabled to handle trains appreciably heavier than those the standard class 11B simples could tackle and in performance they were comparable with the heavier class 11D.

For one job in particular the class 11S became available at just the opportune moment. The former French owned Rosario to Puerto Belgrano Railway was absorbed by the Southern on nationalization, in so far as the southern half of its line was concerned, the northern half going to the Central Argentine Railway. This railway consisted of a single main line linking the city of Rosario, 300 km north of Buenos Aires, with Puerto Belgrano which is the principal naval base in Argentina, close to Bahía Blanca, and normally carried a considerable volume of goods and livestock traffic. As it was built after most of the numerous lines running east to west, it had to leapfrog these by overbridges, which meant that its normal level trajectory was broken at intervals by short sharp gradients which of course had an effect on the motive power in use.

This motive power as handed over consisted of a limited number of elderly locomotives of French design, built to metric measurements, which had nothing in common with the Southern stock. Without exception all required heavy repairs, but literally no spare parts were available, so within a very short time they all had to be put on one side.

Various Southern engines were tried out on those services and after due study it was found that the class 11S was the most successful. This was a striking example of how veterans over 60 years of age were transformed into useful modern units, although with their original boilers, frames, wheels and many other parts. In 1960 No. 4094 made a sea voyage to work on an isolated stretch of line in Patagonia, but the remaining seventeen were still hard at work on the Southern Railway in mid 1967.

CLASS 12—FIG. 21

These 4-6-0 two-cylinder mixed traffic engines constituted the most numerous class ever owned by the Southern Railway, their total being 114. Like the 2-8-0s of classes 11 and 11A they also had numerous practically identical counterparts on the Western and Central Argentine Railways. Nos. 3601 to 3666 were built by Beyer Peacock in 1905-07. Nos. 3667 to 3696 were built in Germany in 1907 as the British builders were overloaded and could not meet the required delivery. Finally Nos. 3697 to 3714 were built by the Vulcan Foundry in 1907-08.

The rate at which the Southern Railway was expanding at that time can be realized from the requisition over a period of three years of more than 200 new locomotives, including in addition to class 12, classes 8A, 8B, 11, 11A, 12A, and 12B.

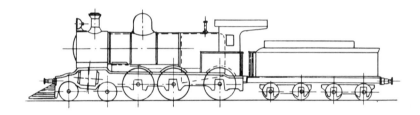

Fig. 21 Class 12 2 cyl. Comp. mixed traffic 3601-3714

The Beyer Peacock class 12's had the Von Borries automatic intercepting valve in the smokebox, while the later ones had the valve on top of the HP cylinder, controlled by the reversing lever. The HP cylinder was 19 in diameter and the LP $27\frac{1}{2}$ in diameter with a stroke of 26 in.

The coupled wheels were 5 ft 8 in diameter and the working pressure 200 lb/in^2.

As was to be expected practically every running shed on the system had one or more class 12's on its strength, and they were to be found on every kind of job at one time or another. In due course a number were superheated, this involving a new HP cylinder with piston valves and new tube-plates. Oil burning equipment was also fitted in a number of cases.

They were always very economical engines to operate and repair and in passing it should be mentioned that they had particularly massive solid bronze axleboxes and big-end bearings which ensured trouble-free service from these components.

In time however, the volume of duties for which they and the other compounds were suitable became progressively smaller, so ways and means were studied for improving the performance of what were in so many respects excellent machines. First came the conversion to simple of ten engines, reclassified 12F, in 1934-5. Next was the use of existing class 12 boilers for the new class 12G in 1937-8, fifteen in all. Finally, in 1948 the conversion of thirty-five further engines to simple, class 12P, was commenced.

Although none now remain in their original form, nearly half of the class, with original boilers, and many other original parts, continue to render excellent service after a life of 60 years and over.

CLASS 12A—FIG. 22

This class of thirty-two two-cylinder 4–6–0 compounds was in effect an enlarged class 12 intended for main-line passenger duties. Nos. 3801 to 3820 came from Beyer Peacock in 1907 and Nos. 3821 to 3832 from the North British Locomotive Co. in 1907-08.

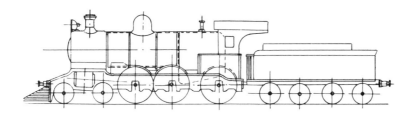

Fig. 22 Class 12A 2 cyl. Passenger originally comp. 3801–3832

The coupled wheels, for the first time on the Southern Railway if one discounts the old class 5 singles which were withdrawn in 1924, were of the relatively large diameter of 6 ft 0 in which has since been the standard for passenger engines. Express passenger services in the true sense of the word, were at last becoming a requirement on the Argentine railways at this time.

The cylinders, bogies, tenders, and many other parts were as in class 12. The boiler barrel was 12 ft $2\frac{3}{4}$ in long and the firebox 7 ft 5 in long as in class 12, but the outside diameter was increased from 5 ft 0 in to 5 ft $4\frac{1}{2}$ in, the working pressure being 200 lb/in^2 for both classes.

As was to be expected the main-line passenger traffic was entrusted to the class 12A and from all accounts they proved adequate. When the new simple engines class 12D first appeared in 1915, however, it was at once evident that they were superior in every respect, and at the same time the very heavy trains then being called for were not suitable for two-cylinder compound haulage.

The conversion of class 12A to simple, therefore, was commenced in 1922 and completed in 1926, superheaters and oil burning equipment being fitted at the same time. As converted, their tractive effort was the same as for class 12D, 20 858 lb at 80 per cent boiler pressure, but in spite of this they were still incapable of a performance equal to that of the class 12D, so for the most part they were relegated to duties of secondary importance.

About 1936 an attempt was made to improve matters by fitting the class 12A with Gooch motion, which made them better, but still not all they should have been. They were again investigated in 1948 at the time of the motive power crisis, already mentioned under class 11S, and poor steam production was found to be the main problem.

The steam and exhaust pipe arrangement was studied and re-designed on the same lines as that applied with great success on the class 12 conversions to class 12P and trials with the first engine so modified proved that it could at last handle anything a class 12D could.

The time spent on studying the problems of exhausting as well as applying steam has often been repaid.

The whole class was therefore modified and in mid-1967 the thirty-two sixty year old 'ugly ducklings' were still to the fore, giving quite a good imitation of the 'swans' they were originally intended to be.

CLASS 12B—FIG. 23

This class of 4-6-0 four-cylinder balanced compound passenger engines was quite different from anything previously built for the Southern Railway. There were nine in all, Nos. 3891 to 3899.

About 1905 the Vulcan Foundry built for the Great Northern Railway of England, a four-cylinder balanced compound 'Atlantic', No. 1300 and the Southern Railway authorities, faced by the ever increasing weight of their passenger trains, were so impressed by the results in service with No. 1300 that they decided to order something very similar. The class 12B compounds, built by Vulcan in 1906 were the result.

The HP cylinders were 14 in diameter and the LP cylinders 23 in diameter with a stroke of 26 in. These were the same sizes as in GNR No. 1300. The coupled wheels were 6 ft 0 in diameter, the Southern standard size for passenger engines. The boiler, however, was not standard with any existing type. The barrel was 14 ft $4\frac{1}{2}$ in long by 5 ft 1 in diameter, and the firebox was 7 ft 9 in long. The class 12A, 12D, 8E boiler was 12 ft $3\frac{3}{4}$ in long by 5 ft $4\frac{1}{2}$ in diameter and the firebox was 7 ft 5 in long. In later years the class 12B boiler was incorporated into the design of the three cylinder 2–8–0 goods engines class 11D.

As in other balanced compounds the inside LP cylinders drove on the leading coupled axle while the outside HP cylinders drove on the second coupled axle. As far as can be ascertained the class 12B did very well on the heaviest passenger services for a number of years but their many moving parts called for careful maintenance.

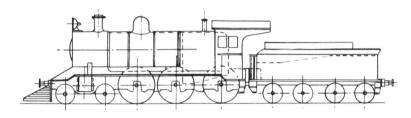

Fig. 23 Class 12B 4 cyl. Comp. Passenger 3891–3899

They were in due course equipped for oil burning and about 1924 superheaters began to be applied. The existing HP cylinders with outside-admission piston valves were retained and at first the superheated engines gave trouble due to leakage of the HP valve spindle packing. A re-designed form of stuffing box and packing was therefore fitted and the trouble was eliminated.

In 1937 it was decided to withdraw these compounds as such from service, due principally to the amount of maintenance they required. From a book-keeping point of view they were converted to the new class 12H but in actual fact only the tenders reappeared as class 12H, the whole of the actual engines of that class being completely new. Some of the original class 12B boilers, however, were still in good condition and six of the total of nine were fitted on 2–8–0 goods engines class BA between 1937 and 1940.

The class 12B was one of the many cases that have occurred of a design which was claimed to and probably did improve performance and produce fuel economy having to be discarded because of the adverse effect on maintenance brought about by its complication and multiplicity of parts, this being particularly applicable on a railway system such as that of Argentina, where the widely scattered sheds make close supervision of maintenance work very difficult.

CLASS 12C—FIG. 24

This class of 4-6-0 goods engines scarcely comes within the scope of this work, as by 1924 all but two had been withdrawn. The two survivors, Nos. 3993 and 3998, however, lasted a long time. The latter was scrapped in 1946, but No. 3993 which for many years was a works shunter at Escalada, carried on quite efficiently for several years more.

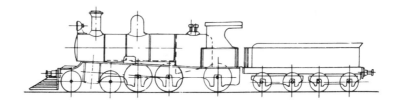

Fig. 24 Class 12C 2 cyl. goods 3991-3999

The class of ten engines, Nos. 3990 to 3999 was built as two-cylinder compounds by Beyer Peacock in 1891. By 1922 all still in service had been converted to simples.

As simples the cylinders were 18 in × 26 in, coupled wheels 4 ft $7\frac{1}{2}$ diameter, and working pressure 150 lb/in^2.

They did good work in their time until outclassed by the general growth in weight of the trains.

CLASS 12D—FIG. 25

These twenty two-cylinder simple superheater 4-6-0 express passenger engines Nos. 3951 to 3970 were built by Beyer Peacock in 1915-17. They were a big advance on any other passenger type, the mainstay of the passenger services until their arrival being the class 12A, which were still two-cylinder compounds.

As originally built the cylinders were 22 in × 26 in, coupled wheels 6 ft 0 in diameter and working pressure 150 lb/in², this relatively low pressure being customary in the early days of superheating when they were built. Walschaerts valve gear was fitted. They quickly showed themselves masters of any job entrusted to them. At this time the seaside resort of Mar del Plata, 400 km from Buenos Aires, was developing by leaps and bounds, and pending the construction of the highway which took place some years later, the train services had to cope with practically the whole of the very large tourist traffic. Though the track in question is mainly level there are two very severe slacks permanently in force for sharp curves and at least one stop for water was normal. After Altamirano, 88 km from Buenos Aires, the track is single and staff exchanging called for some additional speed restrictions. An overall time of $5\frac{1}{4}$ hours, therefore, was no easy task with trains often exceeding 550 tons. The 12D's handled this traffic most successfully until superseded by the class 12E Pacifics from 1928 onwards. They were of course equipped for oil burning.

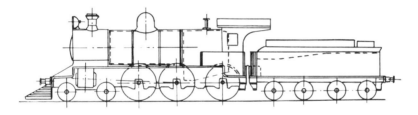

Fig. 25 Class 12D 2 cyl. Passenger 3951–3970

Beginning in 1936 a start was made with a modification which transformed these splendid engines into really superlative machines. Cylinders 19 in × 26 in were fitted, with long-travel piston valves and the working pressure was increased to 200 lb/in². In their new form they proved some of the most economical and trouble-free engines on the system.

After their displacement from the Mar del Plata services they were allocated to other heavy and important services, such as those on the Rio Negro line from Bahía Blanca to Neuquen (554 km) and south from Bahía Blanca to Patagones (274 km) and San Antonio (473 km) where working conditions were far from easy, and on these they gave the greatest satisfaction.

In 1948 when the class was over 30 years old came their finest hour. At that time the national authorities desired to put on a week-end 'propaganda' service, non-stop to and from Mar del Plata, at an average speed of 53.3 miles per hour, with a gross trailing load of up to 450 tons. The 12E's were all fully occupied on other and heavier services, so the choice boiled down to a 12K two-cylinder 4-6-2 or a class 12D 4-6-0. After careful trials a 12D was chosen and in practice this choice was a happy one, their trouble-free reputation being of primary importance. An account of this service, with a photograph of No. 3953 appeared in the *Railway Magazine* of June 1950.

In mid 1967 the class was still intact and performing much useful work.

About 1936 the practice of naming passenger engines was adopted. Class 12D engines were most appropriately named after Argentine birds, as follows:

3951 *Jilguero*	3961 *Mirlo*
3952 *Tordo*	3962 *Condor*
3953 *Churrinche*	3963 *Aguila*
3954 *Chajá*	3964 *Flamenco*
3955 *Chorlito*	3965 *Martineta*
3956 *Ruiseñor*	3966 *Cardenal*
3957 *Charrúa*	3967 *Calandria*
3958 *Picaflor*	3968 *Gaviota*
3959 *Golondrina*	3969 *Zorzal*
3960 *Ñandú*	3970 *Garza*

The name plates were brass castings, carried on the cab sides.

CLASS 12E—FIG. 26

On looking over the history of the numerous classes of locomotives in the fleet of a large railway like the Southern, it is not an easy matter to affirm which was the best class. Nevertheless, most mechanical and operating staff who worked with them would probably agree that this title was worthily earned by the class 12E.

The class consisted of twenty-one engines Nos. 3911 to 3931 of which twenty were built by the Vulcan Foundry in 1927-8. An additional identical engine No. 3931, was built specially by Vulcan for exhibition at the British Trade Fair held in Buenos Aires in 1931.

These were 4-6-2 three cylinder simple superheater oil burning express passenger engines with large coupled wheels 6 ft 6 in diameter. The two outside cylinders were 19 in diameter and the inside cylinder $17\frac{1}{2}$ diameter with a stroke of 26 in. The boiler barrel was 5 ft 8 in diameter, grate area 29.3 square feet and working pressure 200 lb/in². Other main dimensions are given in Table 1. They were fitted with Weir pumps and feed water heaters when built, but these were removed subsequently.

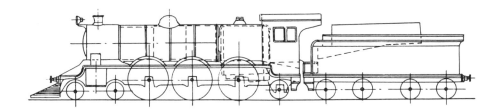

Fig. 26 Class 12E 3 cyl. Express Passenger 3911–3931

From the moment of their arrival it was clear that they could tackle successfully any passenger job the railway had, or was likely to have, and so it has been proved over the years.

During the 1930s various attempts to improve their efficiency still further were made, all of which succeeded to some extent. Some engines were fitted with all three cylinders $17\frac{1}{2}$ in diameter, with long-travel valves, and most of the class received double blast pipes and chimneys. At the request of the footplate staff smoke deflectors were fitted as the engines always appeared to be working well within capacity with a light exhaust which affected visibility.

In 1936 four engines, Nos, 3913, 3914, 3921, and 3930 were fitted with a Western Railway class 15 type of boiler as later adopted on the Southern for their classes 12K, 15A, and 15B. This was of the same diameter as the original, but with a larger firebox with sloping throat and back plates, and with the grate area increased to 32.6 square feet. This change was useful in providing four spare boilers for the remainder of the class and also for the more numerous class 11C goods engines. The results with either type of boiler were uniformly good.

From time to time there was some anxiety over the crank axles, but no serious breakages took place. Up to 1951 at least, careful periodic deflection tests ensured that any axle showing signs of fatigue was renewed, but this was only necessary after something over a million kilometres had been run.

Otherwise the 12E's have always been light on maintenance for three cylinder engines and monthly mileages as the result of long through runs were consistently high. The Bahía Blanca night express sometimes loaded up to 20 vehicles, mostly heavy sleeping and restaurant cars and at times 800 tons of train constituted the nightly task of the 12E's.

During the 1966-7 summer season these engines evidently merited more confidence than did some of the more modern diesels as they were to be seen daily on expresses to and from Mar del Plata, Bahía Blanca, Tandil, etc, apparently none the worse for their forty years. All were still on the books in mid 1967.

They were named, with one exception, No. 3911, after historic personages of the Argentine armed forces, as follows:

3911 *Mar del Plata*	3922 *General Güemes*
3912 *Almirante Brown*	3923 *General Balcarce*
3913 *General Pueyrredón*	3924 *General Alvear*
3914 *General Necochea*	3925 *General Rondeau*
3915 *General La Madrid*	3926 *Coronel Brandsen*
3916 *General Guido*	3927 *General Las Heras*
3917 *General Julio A. Roca*	3928 *General Urquiza*
3918 *General Bmé. Mitre*	3929 *Coronel Pringles*
3919 *Coronel Dorrego*	3930 *Genral Belgrano*
3920 *General Lavalle*	3931 *General San Martin*
3921 *General José C. Paz*	

CLASS 12F—FIG. 27

This class consisted of ten class 12 compound 4-6-0s converted to simple and renumbered 3851 to 3860 in 1934-5. They were fitted with two cylinders 19 in × 26 in and Gooch motion. The working pressure of 200 lb/in^2 was retained and the tractive effort at 80 per cent pressure was increased from 19 039 lb to 22 080 lb. They were of course superheated and equipped for oil burning.

As converted the engines proved very successful in handling fruit and petroleum trains on the Bahía Blanca to Neuquen line with a performance well above what they were capable of in their original form.

About 1955 the delivery was expected of a batch of diesels to help out on the Buenos Aires suburban services with the result that the class 8E engines were more neglected than ever, this being at a time when maintenance had fallen to a very low level. To save the situation pending the arrival of the diesels several

12F's were brought in to work the Buenos Aires to La Plata trains which they did in a most competent manner, but with the disadvantage that they had to be turned at the end of each run.

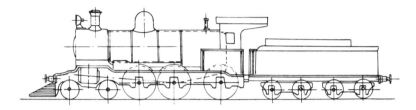

Fig. 27 Class 12F 2 cyl. Mixed traffic 3851–3860

Subsequently they were withdrawn gradually as heavy boiler repairs became necessary, but two were still in service in mid 1967 after a life of over 60 years.

CLASS 12G—FIG. 28

In 1936 there was a definite need for more second-line passenger engines but the situation at the time made it impossible for additional capital expenditure to be contemplated. A solution was found, however, which had the result of providing in effect fifteen new 4–6–0 engines class 12G and nine new 4–6–0 engines class 12H.

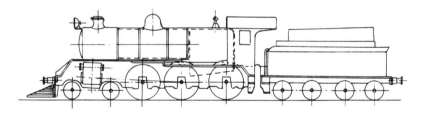

Fig. 28 Class 12G 2 cyl. Passenger 3870–3884

Twenty-four sets of new 4–6–0 chassis complete with cylinders, motion, wheels, etc, were ordered from the Vulcan Foundry as replacements. As far as the class 12G was concerned, the replacements were of fifteen class 12 compounds due for withdrawal. The existing class 12 boilers were fitted on the new chassis and the class 12 tenders were used to complete the job. The result was a very good free running passenger engine for secondary main line work and mixed traffic duties.

The new chassis had cylinders 19 in × 28 in with long-travel valves. The coupled wheels were the standard 6 ft 0 in size for passenger engines.

This work was carried out at the Liniers workshops of the Buenos Aires Western Railway in 1938, as at that time both railways were under one joint administration.

In 1939 engine No. 3870 was fitted with a larger boiler of class 12H type with suitable modifications, but no others were so dealt with. In mid 1967 the class was still intact.

Names of animals found in Argentina were given to class 12G as follows:

3870 *Huemul*	3878 *Venado*
3871 *Aguará*	3879 *Vicuña*
3872 *Guanaco*	3880 *Jaguar*
3873 *Hurón*	3881 *Liebre*
3874 *Mataco*	3882 *Coati*
3875 *Nutria*	3883 *Ardilla*
3876 *Ocelote*	3884 *Ciervo*
3877 *Puma*	

CLASS 12H—FIG. 29

As mentioned in connection with class 12B these nine class 12H 4-6-0s Nos. 3901 to 3909 were officially considered as replacements of the first named four cylinder compounds.

Apart from the nine complete new chassis built by the Vulcan Foundry in 1937, identical with the fifteen for class 12G, new boilers were also built by the same makers. These were of a new type for the Southern Railway, having the barrel 5 ft $4\frac{1}{2}$ in diameter by 12 ft $2\frac{3}{4}$ in long as in classes 12A and 12D, but with a firebox length increased from 7 ft 5 in to 9 ft $0\frac{3}{4}$ in. The throatplate was inclined so as to provide a form of combustion chamber, so the grate area of 25 square feet remained the same.

As in the class 12G the cylinders were 19 in diameter by 28 in stroke, this being the first application of a stroke greater than 26 in.

The assembly of these new engines was carried out at the Liniers workshops in 1938. As they were intended for main-line passenger work they were given high-capacity tenders from goods engines class 11C which in turn received the tenders from the withdrawn class 12B compounds.

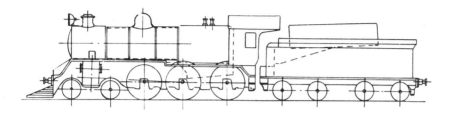

Fig. 29 Class 12H 2 cyl. Passenger 3901–3909

The class 12H were good engines, but in spite of their slightly higher tractive effort, were not quite up to the standard of class 12D as regards actual performance. All were still in service at mid 1967 and were named after former Argentine presidents and political personages as follows:

3901 *Avellaneda*
3902 *Larrea*
3903 *Moreno*
3904 *Sarmiento*
3905 *Alberti*

3906 *Azcuénaga*
3907 *Chiclana*
3908 *Laprida*
3909 *Castelli*

CLASS 12K—FIG. 30

These twelve two-cylinder 4-6-2 passenger engines Nos. 3939 to 3950 were built by the Vulcan Foundry in 1939. They were intended for working heavy stopping trains on the main lines.

The cylinders were 19 in × 28 in and the coupled wheels 6 ft 0 in diameter. The boiler was of a new type, subsequently used on classes 15A and 15B also, with a barrel 5 ft $7\frac{1}{2}$ diameter by 13 ft $3\frac{1}{2}$ in long, the same as had been applied earlier to the 1500 class of 4-8-0 mixed traffic engines on the Western Railway. The firebox was 11 ft $3\frac{1}{2}$ in long with a sloping throatplate forming a combustion chamber 1 ft $9\frac{1}{2}$ in long. The grate area was 32.6 square feet and the working pressure 225 lb/in². These boilers were excellent steam producers and the class did all that was required of it very efficiently. On the faster schedules, however, they did not prove as speedy as was to be expected.

When the 4-8-0s of class 15B with 5 ft 8 in coupled wheels were delivered in 1948-9 it was found that they were more free-running than the 12K's and on examination of the cylinder drawings it was found that in the newer class the exhaust passages had been re-designed to provde a more streamlined path for the steam. Engine No. 3939 of class 12K was therefore fitted in 1950 with cylinders from the 15B patterns and immediately an improvement in its capacity for speed

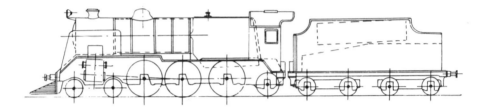

Fig. 30 Class 12K Express Passenger 3939-3950

was apparent. On a trial run on the Bahía Blanca day express with a load of over 400 tons a speed of 115 km/h was maintained with the greatest of ease. Steps were therefore taken to provide new cylinders for the whole class.

These engines had smoke deflectors when built but these were removed subsequently. They also had an exhaust steam injector on the fireman's side which was inclined to be temperamental in the hands of inexperienced men.

The class were all in service at mid 1967.

They were named after Saints, as follows:

3939 *San Juan*	3945 *San Carlos*
3940 *San Luis*	3946 *San Rafael*
3941 *San Matias*	3947 *San Roque*
3942 *San Francisco*	3948 *San Ramón*
3943 *San Antonio*	3949 *San Lorenzo*
3944 *San Pedro*	3950 *San José*

CLASS 12L—FIG. 31

The five engines of this class allocated to the Southern Railway formed part of an original order for ninety placed with the Vulcan Foundry shortly before the nationalization of 1948. Only forty were eventually delivered, the balance being taken in the form of twenty-one metre-gauge 1000 h.p. English Electric-Vulcan diesel-electric locomotives, which it may be said in passing, proved to be the most successful type amongst the thousand or more heterogenous diesels acquired up to 1967.

The class 12L engines were three-cylinder 4–6–2s with cylinders 20 in × 26 in, coupled wheels 6 ft 3 in diameter and a tractive effort at 80 per cent working pressure of 35 830 lb. The taper boiler had a wide firebox with 43 square feet of grate area and the working pressure was 225 lb/in^2. Caprotti valve gear was fitted.

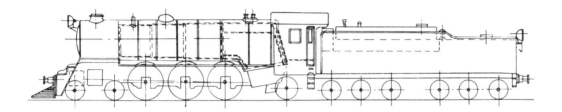

Fig. 31 Class 12L 3 cyl. Express Passenger 3001–3005

The engines were an up-to-date version of a type that had been used most successfully for over twenty years on the heaviest and fastest services on the Central Argentine Railway.

In this latest batch a new design of tender, of enormous proportions, was provided. It was carried on two three-axle cast-steel bogies and weighed just over 103 tons in working order, 3 tons more than the locomotive. This design was intended for services in the Northern provinces served by the Central Argentine Railway where water is both scarce and bad. The water capacity was 9000 gallons and the oil fuel capacity 11$\frac{1}{2}$ tons.

Only five of these engines, Nos. 3001 to 3005, were allocated in 1950 to the Southern (then General Roca) Railway, and they were not received with great enthusiasm as they were so different from normal standards on that railway. There was really no service which called for the haulage of such huge tenders. The Caprotti valve gear reintroduced the spare parts problem which years earlier had been experienced with the four engines of class 15A so fitted.

They were used on the Tandil passenger services for a time, but though still on the books in mid–1967 they had done very little work for some years previously. Names of Argentine lakes were given to four engines, as follows:

3001 *Lago Nahuel Huapi*
3002 *Lago Traful*
3003 *Lago Mascardi*
3004 *Lago Moreno*

CLASS 12P—FIG. 32

This class originated as the result of the motive power shortage of 1948. The class 12 compounds in their original form had become quite inadequate for most modern service requirements, but potentially they were useful engines. Bearing in mind the success of the conversions to simple as class 12F it was desired to augment this series but it was not possible at the time to undertake the manufacture of the Gooch motion with which the 12F's were fitted, nor was it considered that this equipment in itself had contributed much to the success of the class.

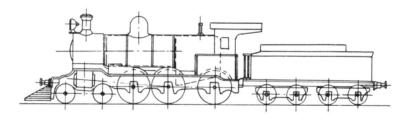

Fig. 32 Class 12P 2 cyl. Mixed traffic 3201-3235

As a legacy from the good old days of plenty there existed a useful reserve stock of class 12 HP cylinders with piston valves, these being symmetrical castings which could be used on the LP side if necessary. A class 12 engine, No. 3624, was therefore fitted with one of these in place of the LP cylinder and the eccentrics and existing valve gear were altered to suit. A new blast pipe made of cast brass was specially designed to improve the steaming qualities and in service the converted engine, now renumbered 3201, quickly demonstrated its ability to handle traffic normally worked by the larger class 12A and 12D 4-6-0s.

Further conversions were put in hand and eventually reached a total of thirty-five, Nos. 3201 to 3235, thus forming a most valuable addition to the second-line strength and releasing larger engines for more important duties.

As an example of their capabilities, No. 3207 on one occasion was pressed into service at Empalme Lobos to take over a main-line train the engine of which had failed. With this train consisting of 62 axles and weighing 573 tons, fourteen minutes were gained on schedule over the 144 miles to Olavarría, including three booked stops en route. While it is true that the average speed of just under 35 miles per hour is not high by British standards, it must be borne in mind that this run was made over a single line involving numerous crossings and that the station working is usually slow on account of the amount of parcels and perishable traffic that has to be handled on these trains.

Whereas the class 12 compounds were averaging about 3000 to 3500 km per month, the class 12P average rose to from 8000 to 10 000 km per month.

In mid 1967, having passed the 60 year mark (they consisted of a very high proportion of the original class 12's of 1905-07 including the boilers) the 12 P's were all in active service and were extremely popular with the footplate and traffic staff. They showed once more the basic soundness of British workmanship and design, and proved that, irrespective of age, such units can be converted to a state of greater efficiency by the application of modern principles.

CLASS 14—FIG. 33

These twelve very large and powerful 4-8-2 + 2-8-4 Garratt engines Nos. 4851 to 4862 were ordered to cope with the rapidly growing grain traffic in the area served by the Bahía Blanca North Western Section, and particularly on the Toay line where track conditions were poor and on which the existing heavy goods engines class 11C with their 16 ton axle loading were not permitted to operate. The Garratts with only $12\frac{3}{4}$ tons maximum axle load were eminently suitable for this work. They were built by Beyer Peacock & Co. in 1929.

The four cylinders were $17\frac{1}{2}$ in × 26 in and the coupled wheels were 4 ft $7\frac{1}{2}$ in diameter. The very large boiler was 6 ft 3 in diameter by 12 ft 3 in long and the

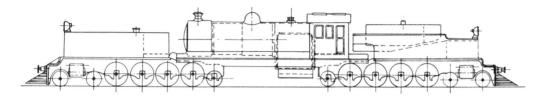

Fig. 33 Class 14 Garratt Goods 4851-4862 (Not to same scale)

grate area was 44.2 square feet. The working pressure was 200 lb/in² and the tractive effort at 80 per cent boiler pressure was 45 910 lb.

These engines were equipped for oil burning in accordance with the general practice for main-line engines. They were able to handle trains of hitherto unprecedented weight, in fact, they could probably have handled even longer trains but for the restricted length of a number of crossing loops.

Apart from the Toay line they also worked on the main Bahía Blanca North Western line to Pico, and also between Tres Arroyos and Bahía Blanca on the Southern Railway proper.

In 1931 for book-keeping reasons, five engines Nos. 4858 to 4862 were transferred to the BBNW stock list and renumbered 4826 to 4830, but they continued to work indiscriminately on any suitable job on either line.

Maintenance was inclined to be heavy due in part to the extremely sandy nature of the region in which they worked and the consequent abrasive action on all exposed moving parts.

They were all at work at the time of the nationalization in 1948, but several years later they were all gradually withdrawn from service. Apart from the maintenance angle, there is no doubt that their comparatively early withdrawal was also due to the fact that as the result of the precipitous decline of freight traffic from about 1954 (due partly to road competition and partly to inefficient operation) there were few, if any, trains of a weight requiring a class 14 to handle them.

During their active life of over twenty years they must have repaid over and over again the amount invested in them, and as has happened in many other countries their performance was in the best tradition of the Garratt design.

CLASS 15A—FIG. 34

This class consisted of eight two-cylinder 4-8-0 mixed traffic engines, Nos. 1550 to 1557. Basically the design corresponded to a series of similar engines built for the BA Western Railway a few years earlier.

The boilers, bogies, and tenders were duplicate with the 4-6-2 class 12K built also by Vulcan Foundry in 1939. The cylinders of class 15A were $19\frac{1}{2}$ in × 28 in compared with 19 in × 28 in for class 12K. The coupled wheels were 5 ft 8 in diameter.

Nos. 1550 to 1553 had Walschaerts valve gear, while Nos. 1554 to 1557 had Caprotti valves and gear. Nos. 1552, 1553, 1556, and 1557 had thermic syphons in the firebox. The engine bogies of both classes 15A and 12K had axles with outside bearings. When built class 15A had the somewhat unnecessary adornment of smoke deflectors which were removed at a later date. Oil burning equipment was fitted.

Extensive tests were carried out to determine the merits or otherwise of the Caprotti valve gear and the thermic syphons, but the results were inconclusive, and in general terms all engines of the series performed in the same excellent manner.

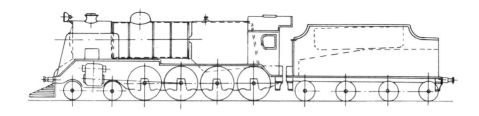

Fig. 34 Class 15A 2 cyl. Mixed traffic 1550–1557

With the outbreak of war in 1939 difficulty soon developed as regards the supply of the numerous spare parts for the Caprotti valve gear, so the four engines so fitted were made standard with the others with new piston-valve cylinders cast in the Escalada workshops and Walschaerts valve gear manufactured there also.

The 15A's were very successful on the heavy Mar del Plata night trains and on fruit trains from the Rio Negro valley and they were capable mixed traffic engines in every sense of the term.

In 1950 one engine was fitted with improved cylinders class 15B which increased their capacity for speed considerably, and the others were dealt with progressively. All were in service in mid 1967, busily engaged on first-class main-line services. They were named as follows:

1550 *Estrella*	1554 *Tronador*
1551 *Lucero*	1555 *Orion*
1552 *Cometa*	1556 *Aconcagua*
1553 *Centella*	1557 *Meteoro*

CLASS 15B—FIG. 35

This was a modernized version of class 15A, being somewhat lighter and thereby having a wider route availability. The main differences were cylinders with stream-lined exhaust passages, inside bearing axleboxes on the engine bogies and lighter tenders having roller bearing axleboxes. Otherwise, the boilers, cylinder size, motion, wheel spacing, etc, were as in class 15A. Thirty of these engines, Nos. 1561 to 1590, were ordered from the Vulcan Foundry just before nationalization and were delivered in 1949.

As had been usual procedure for a number of years, they were shipped fully erected, so their commissioning in Argentina was an easy and speedy matter and it may be mentioned as a tribute to the workmanship put into them that from the first day they gave no trouble whatsoever.

Their arrival was indeed a godsend to the railway because, as has been mentioned earlier, there was a big upsurge of traffic of every kind just after national-ization and no diesels then available to handle a share of it.

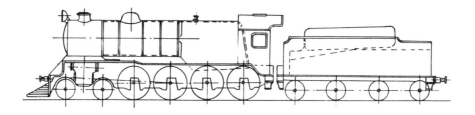

Fig. 35 Class 15B 2 cyl. Mixed traffic 1561-1590

The seasonal fruit traffic from the Rio Negro valley to Buenos Aires over a distance of some 1188 km had been increasing annually and in the years 1950 and 1951 passed the half-million ton mark. This traffic took the form of trains of approximately 1000 tons operated at passenger train timings, mostly over single track. As it had to be dealt with inside a period of three months which also coincided with the summer tourist traffic, and harvest grain movement, it was something of a feat to carry out efficiently.

It can be said without any doubt that the class 15B was the mainstay of the record fruit traffic of 1950 and 1951, and in spite of the advent of diesels of various sizes and shapes, many were still on that job in 1967, by which time, sad to relate, much of the volume of the traffic had been lost to uncontrolled and often inefficient road haulage, the economics of which are impossible to understand, but which by some means or other was able to offer the shippers more attractive rates.

With the possible exception of one or two of the fastest passenger trains, the 15B's have proved more than capable of handling every kind of job throughout the system. They have always been economical on fuel and outstandingly easy on maintenance.

This was the last Southern Railway steam locomotive design, and assuredly it was one of the best.

Main dimensions are given in Table 1.

When new, three engines were given names connected with the then current regime, as follows:

> 1561 *General Perón*
> 1562 *Eva Perón*
> 1563 *Cl. J. F. Castro*

Needless to say, in September 1955 these names were hurriedly removed.

As at mid 1967 there were still no less than 544 of the foregoing Southern Railway locomotives on the books, most of which were in active service or in reserve in serviceable condition once repaired.

This must be one of the largest mass survivals of steam anywhere, and is all the more remarkable in that over 450 engines were anything from 35 to 60 years of age.

7

Locomotives of the Bahía Blanca North-Western Railway

Classes BA, BB, BD, and BE which follow were BA Pacific Railway engines taken over with the Bahía Blanca North Western Railway in 1925.

CLASS BA—FIG. 36

This class comprised eighteen large 2-8-0 goods engines of the Pacific Railway class 1 to 40. Those taken over were Nos. 1 to 6, 17 to 22, and 35 to 40. They were built by the North British Locomotive Co. in 1906-07 and subsequently fitted with superheaters.

The cylinders were 19 in × 26 in and the working pressure was 175 lb/in^2 except for Nos. 1, 4, 18, and 40 which had cylinders 21 in × 26 in and a working pressure of 150 lb/in^2. The coupled wheels were 4 ft 10 in diameter. The majority of the class were at one time or another equipped for oil-burning.

As in the case of the other classes taken over with the BBNW Railway, the BA's worked mainly, but not exclusively, on that railway, and were used as required on the Southern Railway proper, while at the same time various classes of Southern engines were used on the former railway when necessary.

The principal activity of the class BA was the heavy grain traffic on the main BBNW line between Bahía Blanca and Huinca Renancó, but with their 17-ton axle load they could not work on the light track of the Toay line. They were extremely useful engines and economical to operate.

The Pacific Railway suffered more than any other railway in Argentina from bad water and their boilers suffered accordingly, so that a number of the boilers on the engines taken over with the BBNW Railway had boilers which had suffered considerably from the corrosive effects of bad water and their general repairs were costly items. When the class 12B four-cylinder compound 4-6-0s of the Southern Railway were withdrawn in 1937, six of their nine boilers were in good condition and it was found that with very little modification they could be applied to the class BA and thus permit the withdrawal of a like number of badly wasted class BA boilers. Engine No. 2 was accordingly converted in this manner in 1937, Nos. 21 and 36 in 1938, Nos. 17 and 37 in 1939, and No. 35 in 1940.

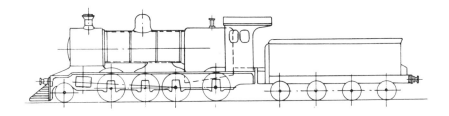

Fig. 36 Class BA 2 cyl. Goods 1-6, 17-22, 35-40

The class 12B boiler was 5 ft 1 in diameter against 5 ft 7 in for class BA, the firebox was 7 ft 9 in long, against 8 ft 0 in, total heating surface was 1690 square feet compared with 1950 square feet, and grate area 28 square feet compared with 30 square feet. On the other hand the working pressure was 200 lb/in^2 as against 175 lb/in^2 on the BA boilers replaced, so the converted engines were quite able to cope with the same duties as previously and by making use of the 12B boilers a heavy expenditure on new BA boilers was avoided. This was a typical example of the principle of strict economy which was forced by circumstances on the British-owned railways after 1930.

The class BA engines were all in service in 1948 but had all disappeared by 1967.

CLASS BB—FIG. 37

This was a class of light 2-8-0 goods engines with a maximum axle load of just under 12 tons, which permitted their use on the light Toay line which was their principal stamping ground. The class consisted of ten engines, Nos. 451 to 462 built by the North British Locomotive Co. in 1906-07. The complete Pacific Railway series was numbered from 451 to 474.

The cylinders were 17 in × 24 in, coupled wheels 4 ft 4 in diameter and working pressure 175 lb/in^2. They were never superheated but were in due course all equipped for oil burning. As can be seen from the diagram, instead of a normal dome they had two openings in the boiler connected by a cylindrical drum, this arrangement being intended to improve steaming and minimize priming on the steep gradients on the Pacific Railway proper.

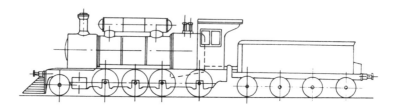

Fig. 37 Class BB 2 cyl. Goods 451–462

With a tractive effort of 18 674 lb at 80 per cent boiler pressure they were powerful engines for working on light 50 lb rail track and they did all that was required of them efficiently.

As with the other ex-Pacific Railway classes, boiler repairs were heavy and at least one complete new boiler was manufactured at Escalada. In 1935 two engines, Nos. 457 and 460, were fitted with boilers in good condition from BA Western engines which had been withdrawn. These boilers were of practically the same dimensions as the ones they replaced and had the same working pressure but had the conventional type of dome. The class lasted until 1948, but heavy boiler wastage caused their withdrawal soon after.

CLASS BD—FIG. 38

These were the BBNW Railway passenger engines belonging to the Pacific Railway class 1032 to 1048. Nine were taken over, Nos. 1032 to 1035, and 1044 to 1048.

They were built by the North British Locomotive Co. in 1905-06 and were essentially designed for secondary main-line and branch-line duties for which they proved quite suitable.

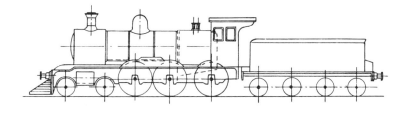

Fig. 38 Class BD 2 cyl. Passenger 1032–1035 & 1044–1048

The cylinders were 19 in × 26 in, coupled wheels 5 ft 7 in diameter and the working pressure was 175 lb/in². They were later superheated by the Southern Railway and equipped for oil burning.

They had a useful but undistinguished life but being a numerically small class which required heavy boiler maintenance they were withdrawn soon after nationalization.

CLASS BE—FIG. 39

These were 0-6-0 inside-cylinder saddle-tank shunting engines from a numerous class, Nos. 2515 to 2568, on the Pacific Railway. The Central Argentine Railway had a large number of practically identical shunting engines.

Fourteen were taken over with the BBNW Railway, four, Nos. 2515 to 2518 built by the North British Locomotive Co. in 1904, six, Nos. 2533 to 2538 built by Kerr Stuart and Co. in 1907, and four, Nos. 2565 to 2568 built by North British in 1914-15.

The cylinders were 16 in × 24 in, coupled wheels 4 ft 1 in diameter and working pressure 160 lb/in². They were never superheated or equipped for oil burning.

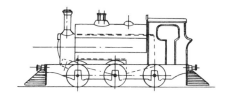

Fig. 39 Class BE Saddle tank Shunter 2513–2518,
2533–2538, 2565–2568

They were extremely handy little engines and before long several found permanent jobs on the Southern Railway where heavier 2-6-2 shunting tank engines predominated.

Nine were still in active service in mid 1967, together with numerous examples of their brethern on the Pacific and Central Argentine Railways.

8

Former State Railway Lines From Patagones to Bariloche (Broad Gauge)

Although these lines were actually only incorporated into the former Southern Railway system from the time of the nationalization of 1948, they were always isolated geographically from the rest of the State Railway network, and as their traffic almost entirely originated on or was handed over by the Southern, they were in an operational sense almost an appendage of the latter.

The broad gauge main line commenced at Patagones, 270 km south of Bahía Blanca where end-on connection was made with the Southern main line, and ran in a westerly direction to Bariloche in the foothills of the Andes, 827 km distant. Through running only became possible in 1936 when the bridge over the Rio Negro at Patagones was opened to traffic.

The line may be divided conveniently into three sections. First, from Patagones to San Antonio, 197 km, the line is on easy gradients and runs through country covered with fairly thick scrub where numerous sheep manage to secure a precarious living.

San Antonio is a fair-sized town on the coast with a growing fishing industry and is where the State Railway had a small but quite well equipped workshop which dealt with all repairs to both broad and narrow gauge stock, the latter being transported to and from Ingeniero Jacobacci on broad gauge wagons.

The second and longest stage is from San Antonio to Ingeniero Jacobacci, 436 km further on. This has always been an exceedingly difficult section to operate as it runs through the most barren and inhospitable country imaginable. Even the scrub is more stunted and sparse than on the previous section and one wonders how the occasional sheep or flock of guanacos seen from the train can possibly keep alive in such surroundings. There are no towns or even large villages and the numerous stops are as a rule only a small cluster of dwellings of railway staff.

Sand blown on to the track by the prevailing high winds is a constant danger and water, save at either end, is practically non-existent. In the days of steam every train had to carry at least one water tank wagon. The adverse gradients in both directions are quite severe and hard work on the part of the locomotives is called for, with flying particles of sand and grit a handicap to be endured at all times.

Ingeniero Jacobacci is a fair-sized village, most of the inhabitants being railwaymen and their families, with a running shed for both broad and narrow gauge engines, as it is from this point that the narrow-gauge line to Esquel commences. This is described in the next chapter.

The final section of 194 km from Ingeniero Jacobacci to Bariloche is a true mountain line as it traverses the most easterly shoulders of the Andes foothills. Characteristically these are treeless and bare, but with a good coating of coarse grass. It is only at Bariloche itself that the first glimpse is had of the glorious scenery of what is aptly termed the Argentine Switzerland.

This final section of the line was only opened as recently as May 1934, the work of building it from Pilcaneyú having been carried out by the Civil Engineers' Dept. of the Southern Railway for account of the Government. Bariloche terminus is 1741 km from Buenos Aires and 827 km from Patagones.

The best express timing was 22 hours for the 827 km at an average speed, including many stops and crossings on the single track, of 38 km per hour.

Dieselization from 1953 has solved many problems, but the line continues to be one of the most difficult to operate and speed restrictions have prevented much improvement on the overall timings.

There is an enormous potential of tourist traffic which at present is unlikely to suffer seriously from road competition, but the cream of the business had by 1967 gone to the airlines, which with Caravelles and Comets take rather less than three hours direct flight from Buenos Aires to Bariloche.

There is practically no bulk goods traffic originating on the line, but fairly heavy shipments of wool and hay are fed in from the narrow gauge line.

There were only two classes of broad gauge locomotives on this line.

CLASS 12M—FIG. 40

These were 4-6-2 two cylinder superheater oil burning mixed traffic engines, used for all kinds of service. There were eighteen in all, Nos. 330 to 342 built by Maffei, Nos. 360, 361, 363, and 364 built by Cockerill, and No. 350 built by St. Pierre. They were built about the year 1921 by which date the section from Patagones to San Antonio had been opened for service.

They were powerful machines with cylinders $19\frac{11}{16}$ in × $24\frac{13}{16}$ in, coupled wheels 5 ft 3 in diameter, working pressure 170 lb/in^2, and a tractive effort at 80 per cent boiler pressure of 20 800 lb. The maximum axle load was only 13 tons. They had bar frames, sandboxes on top of the boiler, and other Continental features. For over 30 years they bore the brunt of the traffic and they proved to be most sturdy and capable.

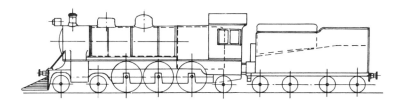

Fig. 40 Class 12M 2 cyl. Passenger 330-342

Being on an isolated section of the State Railway and tending to be forgotten by the central authorities, all manner of makeshift repair jobs had to be carried out to keep them going, as the following example will confirm.

When in 1948 after the Southern took over, the author visited the San Antonio workshops, he was somewhat horrified to see a connecting rod having a completely new big end welded on to it. It was explained, however, that this was no isolated case, and that every rod of the series had had new big and small ends welded on over the preceeding ten years or more without a single breakage in service having taken place.

Another extraordinary happening concerning the class 12M was that just before the outbreak of war in 1939 a batch of coupled wheel tyres was ordered from the USA. These were duly delivered, but apparently someone interpreted the order as an annual one, so for several years, until someone else drew attention to the matter, successive deliveries took place and in 1943 there was a stock of tyres at San Antonio sufficient to have lasted the whole class for over 100 years! Fortunately it was possible eventually to absorb most of the excess on engines of other railways.

The class 12M engines lasted until the advent of the diesels in 1953 after which they were quickly withdrawn.

CLASS 14A—FIG. 41

This class consisted of two enormous Baldwin 2–10–2 tender engines Nos. 500 and 501, of typically American design and construction.

They were built by Baldwin in 1926 and spent their whole life on passenger and mixed trains, latterly on the mountain section between Ingeniero Jacobacci and Bariloche, for which they were eminently suitable, after the line was completed in 1934, prior to which they had worked to what was then the terminus at Pilcaneyú.

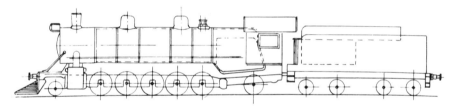

Fig. 41 Class 14A 2 cyl. Goods 500 and 501

They had cylinders 22 in × 26 in, coupled wheels 4 ft 3 in diameter, working pressure 200 lb/in^2, and a tractive effort of 39 281 lb at 80 per cent boiler pressure. The maximum axle load was $15\frac{1}{2}$ tons. They were superheated and equipped for oil burning.

After a life of hard and efficient service they were withdrawn like the class 12M, soon after the diesels appeared in 1953, but during their later years they had some assistance from the Southern classes 11C and 15B, 4–8–0's and 11D, 2–8–0's.

9

The Narrow Gauge Line From Ingeniero Jacobacci to Esquel

This line of 75 cm gauge runs south from Ingeniero Jacobacci on the Bariloche main line to Esquel in the Province of Chubut, 402 km distant. It was first opened for traffic in 1946. The track follows the contours of the Andes foothills and their valleys through good grazing country for sheep, wool being the main item of bulk transport, followed by alfalfa or hay. Gradients in many placed are steep and curves are sharp, the line having been constructed economically with as few large earthworks as possible.

The daily mixed train takes 15 hours for the full journey, or an average of 27 km per hour, but with this including 15 stops, some rather lengthy, and considering the nature of the terrain, this is quite good going for the 75 cm gauge.

The motive power consisted of thirty-six two-cylinder 2–8–2 tender engines having outside frames and equipped for oil burning as follows:

CLASS 75H—FIG. 42

There were twenty-four engines in this class, numbered between 101 and 150, built by Henschel of Germany from 1922 onwards, some having worked on the Patagonian lines before the Esquel line was opened, also on another narrow gauge line from Vinnter, east of San Antonio and subsequently closed.

The cylinders were $11\frac{13}{16}$ in $\times$ $17\frac{5}{16}$ in, coupled wheels 2 ft $7\frac{1}{2}$ diameter and working pressure 170 lb/in^2. The tractive effort at 80 per cent boiler pressure was 10 440 lb. These formed part of a batch of fifty of which twenty-six went to other narrow gauge lines in Patagonia. All were on the books in mid 1967.

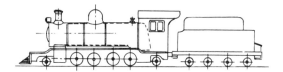

Fig. 42 Class 75H Mixed traffic 75 cm gauge between 101 and 150

CLASS 75B—FIG. 43

There were twelve engines in this class of 2-8-2 tender engines with outside frames, Nos. 1 to 6 and 16 to 22.

All main dimensions were exactly the same as in class 75H but the appearance differed considerably, being obviously of American inspiration, whereas class 75H could easily be identified as being of European origin. The class 75B was built by Baldwin in 1922 for the Patagonian Railway.

For some unexplained reason the Baldwins always seemed to be preferred to the Henschels by the engine crews, but both classes have many years of sterling work to their credit.

Fig. 43 Class 75B Mixed traffic 75 cm gauge 1-6

Winter conditions in the region are extremely severe and operation other than with oil fuel would be no easy matter. Some thought has been given to dieselization but it would obviously be a difficult and expensive matter to produce what would have to be a highly specialized design for the gauge and working conditions. It seems more than likely, therefore, that the classes 75H and 75B or similar replacements will continue to work this line for many years to come.

Until the Southern Railway took over, all heavy rolling stock and locomotive repairs were carried out at the broad gauge workshops at San Antonio, transport to and from that point and Ingeneiro Jacobacci being on broad gauge wagons. In

1950 a start was made to concentrate this repair work at El Maiten, approximately half-way along the line, where there was already a running shed and vehicle repair facilities. As more locomotives existed than were necessary to cover the services, the problem of spare parts was partly solved by cannibalizing a few of these surplus units, which helped materially to speed up the repairs to the remainder.

10

The Agricultural Light Railways

As is well known, during the 1914–18 war the British armies in France were well served in the forward areas by a large network of 60 cm gauge light railways laid on light track, weighing only 20 lb per yard, which if not actually portable was easily transportable in accordance with the ebb and flow of the tide of battle.

The motive power consisted principally of a large number of 4-6-0 side tank engines designed and built by the Hunslet Engine Co. of Leeds. They had cylinders $8\frac{1}{2}$ in x 12 in, coupled wheels 2 ft 0 in diameter and weighed only 14 tons in working order.

What is perhaps not so well known is that, soon after the end of the war, when what was left of this material became surplus, a considerable quantity of locomotives, wagons, track, etc, was purchased by the Southern Railway and put to work in Argentina in the shape of feeder branches to the main line in four localities in the south of the Province of Buenos Aires.

At that time the roads in these areas were extremely bad and in wet weather almost impassable other than by high-wheeled carts hauled by anything up to 25 horses each. Transport costs, particularly for any journey over 10 km or so were therefore somewhat excessive. The idea was that these light railway branches would solve this problem in highly cultivated areas.

The railheads of these areas and the length of lines allotted to each were as follows:

> Balcarce   — 75 km
> Orense   — 73 km
> Copetonas — 47 km
> Cascallares — 56 km

Around Balcarce the crop was mainly potatoes, while in the others it consisted of wheat, oats, barley, and linseed.

Sixteen of the Hunslet 4-6-0 tanks were employed, also thirty-one petrol tractors of Simplex, Baldwin, and Koppell manufacture.

The whole light railway system formed a semi-autonomous section of the Way and Works Department of the Southern Railway, with headquarters and a small workshop at Balcarce, but the engines and tractors from time to time were sent to the Escalada Workshops when particularly heavy repairs were necessary.

The light railways were a valuable asset for over twenty years, but soon after nationalization the general improvement in the roads and the more robust road vehicles then available brought about their gradual suppression.

It is believed, however, that a few of the Hunslet 4-6-0 tanks still survived in 1967 on a light railway in the Province of Corrientes in the far north of Argentina, giving a remarkable life of over fifty years for engines of this type and characteristics.

11

Southern Railway Locomotive Design and Practice

While the basic designs for new locomotives for the British-owned railways were prepared in Argentina, the engineers concerned were always ready to take advantage of the vast store of knowledge and experience of the British manufacturers to whom their construction was entrusted, and also that of their Consulting Engineers in London. Thus they were kept well abreast of contemporary practice at all times. British practice was followed to a large extent, but in some respects local conditions were found to be best met by a departure from the generally accepted ideas prevailing in Britain. The following notes are intended to explain some of these differences and the reasons for them, as well as to give a general idea of Southern Railway practice in a number of directions.

OIL FUEL BURNING

During the period covered by this history, with the exception of the 1939–45 war years, well over 500 of the Southern Railway locomotives used oil fuel, making this railway one of the largest users of oil fuel for locomotives in the world.

Oil has been produced in Argentina for nearly sixty years and the British-owned railways had an interest in one of the companies operating in Comodoro Rivadavia, in Patagonia.

Experiments with the use of petroleum as locomotive fuel took place as early as 1909. With the exception of two years from 1961 during which the armour plating of nationalism was temporarily pierced and foreign companies were contracted to help exploit the oil resources, Argentina has never been quite self-sufficient in oil, but has always had to import a greater or lesser proportion of her requirements. On the other hand, coal suitable for normal locomotive working has not so far been found and consequently all locomotive coal has had to be imported.

It was only natural, therefore, that railways like the Southern should go in for oil burning in a big way, and possibly nowhere else has so much ingenuity and energy been displayed in order to devise the best means of using this type of fuel efficiently and economically.

This involved the correct coordination of the following operations: adjustment of oil feed, adjustment of atomizing steam, adjustment of damper doors, and adjustment of the blower. In most applications of oil-burning equipment each of these operations is separately under the control of the fireman, and this calls for a fair amount of skill and judgement on his part.

In 1921, Mr P. C. Saccaggio, the Chief Mechanical Engineer, devised and patented what was known as the 'combined apparatus' by means of which all four adjustments were made by moving one handle, the proportions of each adjustment having been arranged for in the link up of the apparatus. This system was entirely successful and was adopted as standard, being still in use at the time of writing.

Admittedly a skilled fireman could probably obtain better results with separate controls, but the fact had to be faced that highly skilled firemen were always in a minority and it was considered preferable to forgo the height of perfection obtainable by that minority rather than risk the trouble which could be caused by the inexperienced or careless manipulation of separate controls by the majority.

Contrary to what was believed in some quarters, the use of oil fuel did not cause any increase in boiler maintenance, nor did the maintenance of the equipment itself cause any particular troubles. During the year 1933, out of 261 engine failures only 23 or 8.8 per cent were attributable to the use of oil fuel.

On the other hand, engine availability was greatly increased and longer through runs became possible, such as Buenos Aires to Bahía Blanca via General La Madrid, 680 km, Buenos Aires to Bahía Blanca via Pringles, 640 km, Bahía Blanca to Neuquén, 554 km, and others, the first mentioned being of $15\frac{1}{2}$ hours duration, with stops at all stations. Similar extended workings on goods services produced important economies.

The class 8D shunting engines at the Kilometre 5 marshalling yard were normally in steam from early Monday morning until late on Saturday night, thus giving an availability practically equal to that of diesels, which would never have been possible with the use of coal or wood fuel.

Oil fuel is easy to handle and losses are or should be avoidable, whereas in the case of imported coal, when one considers the losses due to multiple handling, high winds blowing on the stockpiles, pilferage, etc, one wonders just how much of each ton invoiced and shipped ultimately finished up in locomotive fireboxes.

The oil fuel was usually stored in underground tanks into which the incoming tank wagons were emptied by gravity and the oil was pumped to the locomotives as required with suitable heating where necessary.

One or two other adjuncts to oil burning may be mentioned.

It was not customary on the Southern Railway to use a firebrick arch in the firebox, but a suitable refractory lining for the sides and ends of the firepan was of course necessary, as was the flash wall on the firebox back plate. This refractory lining naturally required periodical partial renewal, being composed of separate firebricks, which after the vibration produced by long periods of running tended to work loose.

About 1946 experiments were made with what was called 'super plastic', this being a plastic refractory which was applied cold and could be moulded to any required shape. Before lighting up the boiler, the lining was baked in position with a wood fire for twenty-four hours by which time it had set like cement, and such linings were therefore quite solid and were able to last from one general repair to the next with practically no attention. If any patching had to be done, it was a very simple matter, and the economies obtained by the use of this material were considerable. Unfortunately after nationalization its use was not persisted with as it was naturally higher in first cost than firebricks and the new mentality insisted on always purchasing the cheapest article with little or no thought to quality or true cost in terms of service rendered.

Another useful little gadget on oil-burning engines was the sand gun, consisting of a hand-controlled steam jet, fixed to the firehole door, by means of which a stream of sand could be blown through the tubes from time to time as required, thus keeping them free of soot. As the gun was set on a spherical pivot, all tubes as well as the whole of the firebox tubeplate could be kept clean.

A very complete and detailed record of the Southern Railway system of oil burning exists in the form of a Paper entitled 'The application of oil as fuel for the Modern Locomotive' read before the South American Centre of the Institution of Locomotive Engineers in 1935 by the late Mr W. L. Topham, Paper No. 345, *Journal* No. 128, Nov–Dec. 1935.

STEEL FIREBOXES AND OTHER BOILER DETAILS

As far as the Southern Railway was concerned, the use of steel fireboxes, which from about 1922 became standard practice, produced far better results than did any such fireboxes in Britain, as far as can be ascertained.

In a country like Argentina, where the supplies of water vary in quality from very good to extremely bad, the Southern on the whole was fortunate, though in certain districts the water was far from suitable. Water-softening plants on the base-exchange system were introduced on a large scale from 1936, but even before that the life obtained from steel fireboxes was indeed remarkable. Whether burning coal or oil an average life of 20–25 years was normal.

If anything the life tended to be longer on oil burners as the corrosive effects of wet ashes, etc, round the foundation ring were not met with. Tube life on oil burners also tended to be greater as the tubes did not suffer from the scouring effects of cinders.

As knowledge of and confidence in electric welding increased a gradual approach to all-welded fireboxes was made, and in the later years these became quite numerous and no trouble was experienced with these or with repairs effected by welding. Latterly it was also standard practice to weld all tubes to the firebox tubeplate and to weld all firehole rings in position instead of using rivets, thus eliminating a number of troubles.

As the result of experience with oil burning it became the practice to eliminate the roof stay nuts inside the firebox crown and to rivet over the ends of the stays in position.

Over the years the former standard 'Ramsbottom' safety valves were all replaced by the Ross pop type of valve.

Sellers injectors placed below the cab footstep became standard, having proved the most satisfactory type for local conditions.

As mentioned later, various types of feed pumps, feed-water heaters, and exhaust steam injectors were tried out, some on a considerable scale, but the long-term economies produced were considered insufficient to compensate for the upkeep, and they were gradually discarded.

Blow-down cocks of the gate valve type were standard as the screw type was considered unreliable.

There was a considerable degree of standardization of boilers.

The 5 ft $7\frac{1}{2}$ in diameter boilers of classes 12K, 15A, and 15B were interchangeable, as were those of classes 11C and 12E, the diameter of which was 5 ft 8 in. Classes 8E, 12A, and 12D had boilers of the same dimensions, the diameter being 5 ft $4\frac{1}{2}$ in and the same firebox but shorter boiler barrel fitted class 8A. The same 4 ft 9 in diameter boiler served for classes 7D, 8C, and 8D, while a boiler of the same diameter but with a longer barrel served for classes 11, 11A, 11B, and 11S. The 5 ft 0 in diameter class 12 boiler was also used on classes 12F, 12G, and 12P. Thus, five types of boiler covered eighteen classes of engine.

The introduction of water softening as mentioned earlier, eliminated many of the former troubles, with heavy scaling and priming as well as the corrosive effects of some waters, but as a consequence boiler repair work had to be performed to a very high standard, as there was no longer any formation of scale to cover up potential leakages.

RUNNING GEAR AND OTHER DETAILS

Flangeless tyres. The general practice was as follows:

Six-coupled engines with leading bogie: the first pair of wheels had flangeless tyres (12, 12A, 12D, 12F, 12P).

Six-coupled engines with leading pony: the second, or middle pair of wheels had flangeless tyres (7B, 7D, 8, 8A, 8C, 8D, 8E).

Eight-coupled engines with leading pony: the second and third pairs of wheels had flangeless tyres (11C, 14).

Classes 12E, 12G, 12H, 12K, 15A, and 15B had no flangeless tyres but those which were flangeless for other classes of the same wheel arrangement had tyres with a wider tread and narrower flange than usual.

Piston tail rods Up to about 1933 all new engines had tail rods on their pistons. Experiments were made with various sizes of pistons without tail rods, and as no ill effects were noted all tail rods were gradually eliminated.

Piston valves In 1934 trials were made with the 'Pennsylvania' type of valve head with narrow rings and were so successful compared with the original wide ring type that the former was adopted as standard.

Lighting From about 1928 the old fashioned oil headlamps were replaced by Stones electric lighting sets which also provided some much-needed illumination in the engine cab.

Lubrication For cylinder lubrication the visual hydrostatic type of lubrication was found to be more suitable than mechanical lubricators, being more directly under the control of the drivers.

For motion in general soft grease lubrication became standard. For axleboxes, after trials with oil fed by mechanical lubricators, and with hard grease, the old-fashioned oil box above each axlebox was finally adopted as being most suitable for local conditions.

SPARK ARRESTERS

While oil was the fuel most generally used, there was always a certain number of coal burning engines in use.

During the 1939–45 war when supplies of oil were severely restricted, recourse had to be made to other fuels on a very large scale. These included coal (mainly South African) coal briquettes, wood of various classes, and even briquettes of maize cobs.

In dry weather in Argentina the danger of disastrous crop fires caused by sparks from locomotives is a very serious one.

Mr P. C. Saccaggio in 1922 designed a rotary spark arrester which in practice proved quite fool-proof, definitely impeding the emission of live sparks and in this respect it was far superior to any of the multitude of other arrangements tried out in the country.

In effect, it was a gadget which cost quite a lot to maintain, but this cost was nothing compared to the compensation corresponding to the fires which a less efficient apparatus would have caused.

It may be described briefly as follows: A cross piece having a fixed shaft screwed into its centre was placed in the chimney petticoat near its mouth. This shaft extended down almost to the level of the blast-pipe cap. Ball bearings were mounted at the top and bottom of this shaft and to the outer races of these a tube was fixed. On this tube was mounted what was more or less a conventional conical wire mesh spark arresting basket, which was free to revolve about the shaft on the ball bearings. Motion was imparted by the blower jet or the exhaust steam impinging on the vanes which connected the basket to the tube, which were placed turbine-wise to assist this rotary motion.

While the engine was working the basket revolved at very high speed and while the exhaust gases passed freely, all live sparks were effectively disintegrated and eliminated as a potential source of danger. Entry of sparks at the top or bottom was effectively prevented by suitable baffles.

By fitting collars of various depths to the different classes of chimney petticoats it was possible to adopt one standard size of spark arrester unit to all engines, which proved of particular utility during the war years, when the rate of replacement was necessarily somewhat high.

A small drip-feed lubricator placed on the outside of the chimney fed cylinder oil to the ball bearings and was remarkably effective.

Coal and wood burning engines were in addition fitted with an arrangement for flooding the ashpan en route and thus preventing hot cinders from getting on to the track.

GADGETS

Like many other overseas railways the Southern did its full share of trying out all manner of proprietary gadgets which were claimed to reduce fuel consumption, improve efficiency, etc. Unfortunately, few if any of these either claimed or helped to reduce or simplify maintenance.

Here again local conditions swayed the balance against most of these inventions, because even though they no doubt did produce the economies claimed, their eventual maintenance proved not only costly but troublesome, calling for the stocking of numerous small spare parts, etc, so with few exceptions they were gradually abandoned on those grounds as distinct from any reflection on their efficiency as such.

It must be borne in mind that on a far-flung network like the Southern there were of necessity a considerable number of small running sheds in locations where close supervision was extremely difficult and where the number of high-grade skilled workers employed had to be kept to a minimum, yet the running maintenance of the few engines stationed at each shed depended on the staff on the spot. It was logical, therefore, to follow a policy of adopting all possible steps to ensure that the maintenance work was kept as simple as possible, so that by and large it could be performed successfully by workmen of average rating. It is a matter of record that most of the special appliances tried out in Argentina were also tried out and subsequently discarded by British Railways.

The fact that it was generally possible to ensure that almost 80 per cent of the total steam locomotives fleet were available for service would seem to demonstrate that the practices described in the preceeding pages produced the desired results.

Finally, a few other features differing from British practice may be mentioned. Steam for the blower was taken from a connection on the dome with a pipe leading outside the boiler to the blower valve on the side of the smokebox. This eliminated an internal steam pipe, always a potential source of trouble.

Cowcatchers were an essential piece of equipment. These were made of wood, thus being easily repairable in case of damage. The front buffers on tender engines and those at both ends of tank engines were arranged to fold over backwards (or inwards in the case of hind buffers on tank engines) so that they would not hinder any object struck by the cowcatcher from being thrown clear.

Hand-operated traversing jacks for use in case of derailments were carried on the engine side platforms.

The loading gauge for the Argentine broad gauge railways was a very generous one and many locomotives measured up to 14 ft 6 in from rail to top of chimney, with up to 10 ft 0 in width over cab. Unfortunately, track conditions and axle load restrictions meant that full use of these overall dimensions could not be made in so far as building in all possible power was concerned, as in general a maximum axle loading of 18 tons had to be observed, with even more severe restrictions on many secondary and branch lines.

12

Southern Railway Experimental
Diesel-electric Units

Although this work deals primarily with the steam locomotive stock of the Southern Railway, the contribution made to the development of diesel-electric traction from 1929 onwards was of great importance, and certainly deserves to find a place in any comprehensive history of the evolution of this form of motive power for railway service.

About 1928 the enormous and steady increase of the Buenos Aires suburban services caused the Board of Directors and Mangement to give serious thought to electrification. This would have been a task of great magnitude involving a very large capital outlay, however, and about the same time the hitherto prosperous era on the railways was beginning to show signs of weakening, so there was a natural reluctance to pursue the matter fully until all possible alternatives had been studied. Throughout the world at that time diesel electric traction was for all practical purposes in its infancy. There were, it is true, a large number of experimental units in existence in a number of countries, but few, if any, regular revenue-earning services operated by this form of traction.

Mr P. C. Saccaggio, Chief Mechanical Engineer of the Southern Railway, had already given considerable attention to this matter and he had conceived the idea that it would be possible to design and operate train sets driven by conventional traction motors which would derive their power from diesel engines, and that these trains would enable a service to be rendered which would in every way equal that possible with electrification, yet without anything like the capital outlay involved in the installation of the latter system.

The diesel engine or engines would be installed in a special vehicle called a mobile power house, semi-permanently coupled to one end of the train, which would be composed of what were in effect electric coaches, with their own traction motors, driving compartments, etc, as required.

In principle this idea was considered attractive and received the enthusiastic support of two eminent personalities, Sir Sam Fay and Sir Brodie Henderson, a member of the Board and the Chairman of the railway's consulting engineers, respectively.

As a first step, with the object of acquiring some first-hand experience of diesel-electric traction under local conditions, two small locomotives were ordered, embodying diesel engines and electrical equipment of makes that had already proved their worth. Chassis, body, etc were specified by the railway, embodying,

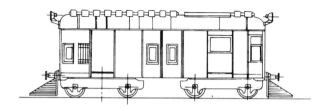

Fig. 44 375 h.p. Diesel Electric CM201

for example, standard carriage and wagon wheels 3 ft $1\frac{1}{2}$ in diameter, standard buffing and drawgear, etc, being what later became known as type B–B with two two-axle bogies.

The two units were built by the Metropolitan Carriage & Wagon Co. and delivered in 1929. The first, No. CM 201 (Fig. 44) was fitted with an eight-cylinder Beardmore diesel engine developing 370 h.p. at 700 rev/min. The choice of engine

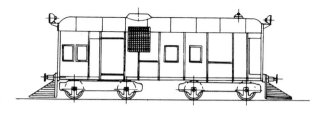

Fig. 45 420 h.p. Diesel Electric CM202

in this case was influenced by the successful performance of this type in railways in Canada and Spain over several years. The second, No. CM 202 (Fig. 45) was fitted with a six-cylinder Sulzer diesel engine developing 420 h.p. at 650 rev/min. There had already been successful experimental applications of the Sulzer engine in Europe. Many tests and trials were made with these two units, both of which displayed a high level of reliability. CM 201 on one occasion made the longest non-stop run hitherto achieved in South America, from Buenos Aires to Neuquén, a distance of 1194 km. This followed other very long successful non-stop runs in Canada made with units powered by the same make of diesel engine.

Both of these units, of course, were too small to take a regular active part in the normal services, but they were tried out on a wide variety of duties and constituted a valuable means of training staff for the larger units which were to follow. In 1941 both were stripped of their power equipment, and made into very useful parcel vans. In the meantime, Mr Saccaggio's designs for his first diesel-electric trains had gone ahead and an order was placed with Messrs Armstrong-Whitworth & Co., for the first two mobile power houses, Nos. UE1 and UE2 (Fig. 46) which arrived in Argentina at the end of 1930.

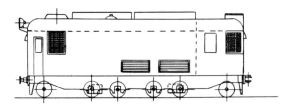

Fig. 46 1200 h.p. Diesel Electric Mobile Power Houses UE1 and UE2

Each was equipped with two eight-cylinder Sulzer diesel engines, each developing 600 h.p. at 700 rev/min. The main generators were made by Oerlikon, and the traction motors by Metropolitan-Vickers. In running order they weighed 92 tons, and the total loaded train weight was 314 tons. They had a pony truck at each end and four fixed axles in the main frame, two of which had traction motors. There was a driving compartment at one end only, as they were semi-permanently coupled to the coach sets at the other end.

The corresponding five-coach train sets had meanwhile been built in the railway workshops at Remedios de Escalada. These were adaptations of the standard carriage design, being large vehicles 82 ft 0 in over buffers, each carried on two two-axle bogies, with one traction motor on each bogie, and with a driving compartment in the end coach. Three were first class with 100 seats in each, and two second class, one with 150 seats and the other with 120 seats plus postal and luggage compartments.

These two trains soon proved that they were capable of doing what had been claimed for them. The outstanding advantage of running a double-ended train in and out of the main terminus at Plaza Constitución was immediately evident, and their capacity for acceleration was superior to that of the average steam train, though in normal working as they had to fit in with steam diagrams this capacity could not be used to full advantage. They were arranged so that they could run in multiple as a ten-coach train with a mobile power house at each end, but usually they were confined to services on the Quilmes line where it was more convenient to work them separately.

Once they had settled down, they worked regularly day in and day out on what must have been one of the very earliest regular services of its kind in the world.

Both trains continued to render good service up to the time of the nationalization of 1948.

The practicability of the mobile power houses having been demonstrated successfully, the next step was the design of three larger units to operate eight-coach trains and thus take a full share of the heaviest and fastest suburban traffic.

In the design of these new mobile power houses, Mr Saccaggio introduced three features which subsequently over the years have become commonplace in diesel locomotive design, but which as far as has been possible to ascertain were hitherto unknown or at least untried in 1931 when the preliminary drawings were prepared. Not being altogether satisfied with the rigid frame arrangement of UE1 and UE2, he arranged for the new power houses Nos. UE3, 4, and 5 (Fig. 47) to be carried on two-axle bogies, this being one of the earliest applications, if not the

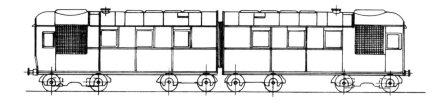

Fig 47 1700 h.p. Diesel Electric Mobile Power Houses UE3, UE4, and UE5

very first, for high-powered diesels. This, of course, is the principle which has been applied to all main-line diesels in the USA and elsewhere since about 1945.

The second feature was the construction of the power houses in two units or halves one with driving compartment and one 'dead', an arrangement which years later became widespread in the USA in particular.

The third notable feature was the use of roller bearings on all axles, which up to that time had been most exceptional. The particular axleboxes used were designed by Mr Saccaggio in association with Messrs. J. Stone & Co., using Skefko bearings, and were widely employed on Southern Railway passenger coaches, including those built to run with the new mobile power houses. To the author's knowledge, some of the original axleboxes were still in service in 1967 after nearly thirty years. Roller bearing axleboxes were a particular boon in the often extremely dusty conditions in Argentina and of course nowadays it would be almost unthinkable to build any type of railway vehicle without this equipment.

The manufacture of UE3, 4, and 5, was again entrusted to Messrs Armstrong-Whitworth & Co., and they were delivered in 1933.

After the good performance of the earlier Sulzer diesel engine this make was specified. Each half unit had one eight-cylinder diesel engine developing 850 h.p. at 550 rev/min making a total of 1700 h.p. per power house. There is no doubt that the low rotational speed was a major factor in the fantastically trouble-free and exceptionally long life of these engines. The main generators were by Brown-Boveri and the traction motors by English Electric, and in both cases full marks are due for quality and reliability.

Each half unit was on two two-axle bogies with two traction motors on each end bogie. The two halves were connected by a flexible gangway.

The weight in working order of each complete power house was 133 tons. Each train was composed of eight coaches of the same design as before but with roller bearing axleboxes. Five first-class coaches provided 500 seats, and three second-class coaches 380 seats, the train weight being 470 tons.

The new trains soon showed what they were capable of and in test runs some acceleration rates and overall running times far superior to anything known hitherto were achieved. In normal service they averaged between 8500 and 9000 kilometres per month.

For the most part their working was fitted in with existing steam diagrams, but for a time a special accelerated diagram employing two of the trains was in force. This allowed for only 5 to 10 minutes turn-round time at terminals, as against 35 to 40 minutes for steam locomotives. This was arranged primarily to demonstrate what could be done if a greater number of similar trains were available, and after a few years to prove the point they reverted to normal diagrams.

The trains were in charge of one motorman and usually carried an apprentice mechanic in the power house.

The three power houses were withdrawn about 1959 after a hard slogging life of over 25 years, which by present-day standards is exceptional for diesel locomotives of more up-to-date design and manufacture, and the feat is a wonderful testimonial to the excellence of their design and construction. The carriages, after being stripped of their electrical equipment, were still mostly in service in 1967.

The impact of the favourable impression produced by the performance of these new trains was weighty enough to bring about the postponement of the projected electrification, although traffic continued to increase and some measures of relief were still as urgently required as ever.

When the administrations of the Southern and Western railways were combined in 1934, the influence of the latter, whose suburban lines were already electrified, was understandably all in favour of that system.

The deteriorating situation of the railways in the early thirties, however, prevented a decision one way or the other, but the controversy of mobile power houses versus electrification continued to be debated at great length right up to the outbreak of war in 1939, with the production of voluminous reports upholding one system or the other, but wartime conditions followed by the pending sale of the railways left the matter still undecided when nationalization took place.

Since then, the national authorities have come to the conclusion that electrification must be faced and detailed studies and projects have been prepared, but the financial outlay involved cannot at present be contemplated in view of the enormous deficit of the railways as a whole.

While Mr Saccaggio's main interest lay in the field of mobile power houses for suburban service, he was well aware of the potential benefits of main-line diesel-electric traction, and when the later three power houses were ordered, he also ordered from Armstrong Whitworth & Co. what was destined to become one of the most remarkable and outstandingly successful diesel-electric locomotives ever built to this day.

This was No. CM 210 (Fig. 48) which entered service in December 1933. Basically, it was a main-line version of the double-unit power houses Nos. UE3, 4, and 5, having the same Sulzer diesel engines and Brown Boveri generators. It carried six English Electric traction motors of 230 h.p. each, however, in place of 134 h.p. motors used on the power houses. A driving compartment was provided at the outer end of each half unit, these being equipped for one-man operation.

Three sets of driving wheels and axles were provided with the locomotive, these having gears of different sizes calculated for express trains, mixed trains, and heavy goods trains services respectively. After extensive trials with all three gear

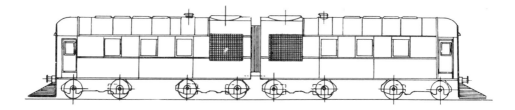

Fig. 48 1700 h.p. Diesel Electric Locomotive CM210

ratios the intermediate set was adopted permanently, as it was found that in this form the locomotive could handle the widest range of normal traffic.

For many years CM 210 ran the heavy night train from Buenos Aires to Bahía Blanca, a distance of 640 km, returning on alternate nights. This train quite often was made up to twenty four-axle vehicles with a weight of 900 tons or over and seldom weighed less than 700 tons. The number of intermediate stops varied throughout the week, but in general an average running speed of rather more than 60 km/h was called for. The punctuality of this service was exemplary, and seldom if ever was a late arrival attributable to any fault on CM 210.

A remarkable feature was the working of this train with one man only in the cab, something which nowadays would be unthinkable. This was no mean feat with a train of such weight, running at night through open country, on a single line with many unprotected level crossings. An average of 13 000 kilometres per month was customary on this service, equivalent to twenty trips.

In 1941/42 in its eighth year of service CM 210 covered 169 726 km in revenue service, an average of 14 144 km per month, over which period the operating costs for diesels worked out at 19.54 cents per locomotive kilometre compared with 41.17 cents per steam locomotive kilometre, maintenance costs being approximately 30 cents in both cases.

CM 210 was still on the Bahía Blanca night expresses until well after the nationalization of 1948 and was only retired in 1960, more due to the lack of spare parts than to general decrepitude. The writer has been unable to trace any record of a remotely comparable main-line service worked regularly by diesel locomotives anywhere in the world during the period 1934-9.

It was hardly surprising, therefore, that, as recorded in a special Overseas number of the *Railway Gazette* of 28 November 1934, the Chairman of the Southern Railway, Sir Follett Holt, at the Annual General Meeting on 7 November of that year, stated that in view of the recent experiments with diesel-electric traction it was unlikely that his Company would again ship a steam locomotive to Argentina. Though Sir Follett's prophecy was not destined to be fulfilled for a good many years, this was due more to influences other than those of a purely technical nature, and it was fully justified by the technical capabilities of the experimental diesel units.

As a further indication that these were indeed well before their time it may be mentioned that in the special issue of the *Railway Gazette* referred to above there was not a single illustration, either with the text or in the numerous advertisements, of a main-line diesel unit except for one photograph of a streamlined three-car high-speed diesel train of the Union Pacific Railway in the United States.

During this experimental period the Southern Railway received four additional main-line diesel-electric locomotives which, however, were not to the railway's design or specifications.

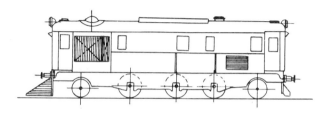

Fig. 49 800 h.p. Diesel Electric Locomotive CM204 and 205

The first two, Nos. CM 204 and 205 (Fig. 49) were built by Armstrong Whitworth & Co., and it was understood at the time that they were originally destined for the 5 ft 6 in gauge lines of the Ceylon Government Railway. They arrived in Argentina in 1937. They were designed to operate together as one 1600 h.p. unit, each being equipped with one Sulzer diesel engine developing 800 h.p. at 700 rev/min. The main generator and traction motors were manufactured by Crompton Parkinson Ltd. They were of the rigid frame design having three driving axles with wheels 4 ft 0 in diameter and a pony truck at either end with 3 ft 0 in diameter wheels. The locomotives were not a great success and after a few years of intermittent service on secondary duties they were scrapped during the war period.

The second two locomotives were also received in 1937 and were of an experimental nature, intended to try out the two-stroke system of diesel engines against the four-stroke engines already in use. They were Nos. CM 206 and 207 (Fig. 50)

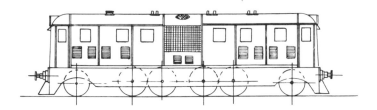

Fig. 50 900 h.p. Diesel Electric Locomotive CM206 and 207

and were built by Harland & Wolff of Belfast. Each locomotive had two 'Harlandic' two-stroke diesel engines developing 450 h.p. at 800 rev/min. The main generators were from Brown Boveri and the traction motors by Lawrence Scott Ltd. They were of the rigid frame type having four driving axles with wheels 4 ft 7½ in diameter and a pony truck with 3 ft 5 in diameter wheels at either end.

When on their best behaviour these were remarkably powerful and speedy locomotives for their size, but unfortunately they were extremely erratic and it soon became evident that at that time the two-stroke type of engine had not yet attained the same degree of reliability in traction service as the contemporary four-stroke type. As an experiment they proved instructive but their performance on regular mainline work was very limited and they also were scrapped during the 1939–45 war period.

Both they and Nos. 204 and 205 at one time or another fell victims of a hazard to which the rigid frame type of diesel locomotive was always vulnerable on the railways of countries like Argentina. In periods of dry weather, straw, grass, and weeds tend to pile around the traction motors and other under-floor fittings and in time this accumulation was apt to become impregnated with fuel or lubricating oil, which seeped through joints or openings in the floor. Due to the sparks from the brake blocks or other causes serious fires were prone to occur, no matter what precautions were taken. In the case of locomotives carried on bogies it was possible to have the engine-room floors entirely oil-proof, thus eliminating all danger of this nature.

In later years there have been numerous developments in diesel traction on what was formerly the Southern Railway, but this is a matter outside the scope of this chapter, the purpose of which is to place on record the outstanding pioneer work conceived and carried out mainly by the late Mr P. C. Saccaggio, to whose name should be added that of his personal assistant for many years, the late Mr Hugh MacIntyre, on whose capable shoulders fell much of the burden of ensuring that the ideas worked out in daily practice, a task which he performed with outstanding dedication and success.

13

Concluding Remarks

Enough has been written to place on record something of the characteristics and performance of the steam locomotives of the Buenos Aires Great Southern, and to round this off a list is given below of those which in July 1967 were still on the active list of the General Roca Railway, to employ its current designation.

Class	Type	Originally Built	Age in Years 1967	Number on Books	Remarks
7D	2cyl 2-6-0	1913	54	21	Class Intact
8A	2cyl 2-6-2T	1906–07	61–60	34	Class Intact
8B	2cyl 2-6-2T	1908	59	10	Class Intact
8C	2cyl 2-6-2T	1913–14	54–53	3	
8D	2cyl 2-6-2T	1914–26	53–41	40	Class Intact
8E	3cyl 2-6-4T	1923–30	44–37	21	
11B	2cyl 2-8-0	1914–32	53–35	99	Class Intact less one
11C	3cyl 4-8-0	1925–9	42–38	75	Class Intact
11D	3cyl 2-8-0	1927	40	35	Class Intact
11S	2cyl 2-8-0	1903–07	64–60	17	Converted from compounds 11 and 11A
12A	2cyl 4-6-0	1907–08	60–59	32	Class Intact
12D	2cyl 4-6-0	1915–17	52–50	20	Class Intact
12E	3cyl 4-6-2	1928–31	39–36	21	Class Intact
12F	2cyl 4-6-0	1905–08	62–59	2	Converted from compounds class 12
12G	2cyl 4-6-0	1937	30	15	Boilers class 12 of 1905–08
12H	2cyl 4-6-0	1937	30	9	Class Intact
12K	2cyl 4-6-2	1939	28	12	Class Intact
12L	3cyl 4-6-2	1950	17	5	Class Intact
12P	2cyl 4-6-0	1905–08	62–59	35	Converted from compounds class 12
15A	2cyl 4-8-0	1939	28	8	Class Intact
15B	2cyl 4-8-0	1948–49	19–18	30	Class Intact
BE	2cyl 0-6-0ST	1904–14	63 53	9	
			Total	553	

Due to the indifferent results obtained from some of the diesel units purchased over the past twelve years and also to the serious financial situation of the railways, whose annual deficit has now reached astronomical levels, it seems safe to predict that the days of steam traction on the Southern Railway are by no means over.

Furthermore, as and when attrition does take place it will not necessarily affect only the very oldest classes, some of which may well outlive the others.

It may happen, therefore, that to one of the veterans on the foregoing list will fall the distinction of being, if not the last, at least the oldest steam locomotive manufactured in Britain to remain in active service.

On those grounds alone it has been considered worth while to make their history available to help to complete the full saga of the unforgettable achievements of the British steam locomotive manufacturing industry.

Diagram No.	Class	Numbers	Quantity originally built	Dates Built	Builders	Type	Cylinders	Coupled wheels	Total heating surface sq. ft.	Grate area sq. ft.	Working pressure lb/sq.in.	T.E. at 80% working pressure, lb	Total weight of engine & tender in working order T.C.Q.	Remarks
1	1	184-195	12	1889	B. Peacock	4-4-2 T	16" × 24"	5'-8"	1069	16.5	150	10 820	53-13-0	Converted from class 6 4-4-0 tender engines
2	1B	143, 174-183	10	1906-06	B. Peacock	4-4-4 T	18" × 24"	6'-0"	1282	22.5	160	13 824	66-4-0	Purchased from B. A. Western Ry. 1929 and 1936
3	3C	2031-2040	10	1902-06	Kitson & Stephenson	0-4-0 T	14" × 21"	3'-2"	475	9.0	160	13 856	26-3-3	Kitson valve gear
4	6B	251-275	25	1897-1904	B. Peacock	4-4-0 2cyl. Compound	17" & 24½" × 26"	5'-8"	1082	17.5	175	12 443	69-0-2	Converted from class 6 4-4-0 simple engines
5	7	3001-3028	28	1885-86	B. Peacock	2-6-0	17" or 18" × 26"	5'-2"	1086	20.13	150	15 050	71-1-3	
6	7B	3071-3098	28	1901	B. Peacock	2-6-0 2cyl. Compound	18" & 26" × 26"	5'-8"	1240	20.13	175	15 139	78-5-0	2 converted to simple 1950 cyl 18" × 26" T.E. 17350 lb
7	7D	3101-3122	22	1912-14	B. Peacock	2-6-0	19" × 26"	5'-8"	1386	22.2	175	19 304	101-10-1	No. 3101 built as compound converted to simple 1926
8	8	3301-3318	18	1898-1903	B. Peacock	2-6-2 T	16" × 24" / 18" or 19" × 26"	4'-7½"	1037	16.5	150	13 280	51-12-0	Converted from class 6 4-4-0 tender engines
9	8A	3321-3354	34	1906-07	N. British	2-6-2 T		5'-2"	1660	27.0	160	19 390	73-15-0	
10	8B	3401-3410	10	1908	Naysmith Wilson	2-6-2 T	17" × 24"	4'-4"	1245	20.3	180	19 200	61-6-1	
11	8C	3451-3491	41	1913-14	Stephenson & N. British	2-6-2 T	19" × 26"	5'-8"	1395	22.1	160	17 700	76-10-0	
12	8D	3501-3510	10	1913	B. Peacock & N. British	2-6-2 T	19" × 26"	4'-7½"	1395	22.1	150	20 300	74-12-0	
12	8D	3150-3179	30	1926										
13	8E	3530-3591	61	1923-30	H. Leslie, N. British & Vulcan	3 cyl. 2-6-4 T	17½" × 26" (3)	5'-8"	1631	25.0	200	28 110	100-19-0	
14	9	351-361	11	1898	B. Peacock	0-6-2 T	16" × 22"	3'-8"	915	15.75	150	15 360	47-11-2	
15	11	4001-4040	40	1903-07	B. Peacock & Vulcan	2-8-0 2cyl. Compound	19" & 27½" × 26"	4'-7½"	1522	24.5	200	23 658	96-3-2	Von Borries type,
16	11A	4041-4070	30	1907-08	Vulcan	2-8-0 2cyl. Compound	19" & 27½" × 26"	4'-7½"	1522	24.5	200	23 658	101-13-0	Semi-automatic type
17	11B	4101-4200	100	1914-32	B. P., German, N.B. & Vulcan	2-8-0	19" × 26"	4'-7½"	1522	24.5	160	21 650	104-14-3	
18	11C	4201-4275	75	1924-29	Armstrong, Vulcan & B. Peacock	3 cyl. 4-8-0	17½" × 26" (3)	4'-7½"	2297	29.3	200	34 400	148-17-1	
19	11D	4301-4335	35	1926-27	Armstrong	3 cyl. 2-8-0	17½" × 26" (3)	4'-7½"	1718	28.0	180	31 000	123-18-2	
20	11S	4080-4097	18	1906-07	B. Peacock & Vulcan	2-8-0	19" × 26"	4'-7½"	1522	24.5	200	27 060	101-13-0	Converted from compound classes 11-11A 1949-65
21	12	3601-3714	114	1905-08	B. Peacock, German & Vulcan	4-6-0 2cyl. Compound	19" & 27½" × 26"	5'-8"	1603	25.0	200	19 309	106-10-2	3601-46 Von Borries type 3647-3714 semi-automatic type
22	12A	3801-3832	32	1907-08	B. Peacock & N. British	4-6-0	19" × 26"	6'-0"	1631	25.0	200	20 858	114-1-2	Originally compound—converted to simple 1929-36

Diagram No.	Class	Numbers	Quantity originally built	Dates Built	Builders	Type	Cylinders	Coupled wheels	Total heating surface sq. ft.	Grate area sq. ft.	Working pressure lb/sq. in.	T.E. at 80% working pressure lb	Total weight of engine & tender in working order T.C.Q.	Remarks
23	12B	3891–3899	9	1906	Vulcan	4-6-0 4cyl. Compound	14″ & 23″ × 26″	6′-0″	1690	28.0	220	23 000	114-14-0	
24	12C	3990–3999	10	1891	B. Peacock	4-6-0	18″ × 26″	4′-7½″	1281	23.2	150	18 214	86-10-0	
25	12D	3951–3970	20	1915–17	B. Peacock	4-6-0	19″ × 26″	6′-0″	1631	25.0	200	20 858	112-4-2	Cylinders originally 22″ × 26″ pressure 150 lb. modified 1936-37
26	12E	3911–3931	21	1927–31	Vulcan	3cyl. 4-6-2	(2)19″(1) 17½″ × 26″	6′-6″	2297	29.3	200	27 425	151-7-0	3913-14-21-30 fitted with class 15A boilers 1936
27	12F	3851–3860	10	1905–08	B. Peacock, German & Vulcan	4-6-0	19″ × 26″	5′-8″	1603	25.0	200	22 080	106-10-2	Converted from compound class 12-1934-35 Gooch motion fitted
28	12G	3870–3884	15	1938	Vulcan (New chassis)	4-6-0	19″ × 28″	6′-0″	1603	25.0	200	22 462	124-16-0	Boilers and tenders from compounds class 12
29	12H	3901–3909	9	1938	Vulcan	4-6-0	19″ × 28″	6′-0″	1651	25.0	200	22 462	139-13-0	Tenders from existing engines
30	12K	3939–3950	12	1939	Vulcan	4-6-2	19″ × 28″	6′-0″	2160	32.6	225	25 270	156-18-0	
31	12L	3001–3005	5	1950	Vulcan	3cyl. 4-6-2	20″ × 26″ (3)	6′-3″	2507	43.0	225	35 830	203-18-0	Central Argentine type. Caprotti valve gear 12 wheel tenders
32	12P	3201–3235	35	1905–08	B. Peacock, German & Vulcan	4-6-0	19″ × 26″	5′-8″	1603	25.0	200	22 080	106-10-2	Converted from compound class 12-1949-65
33	14	4851–4862	12	1929	B. Peacock	4-8-2 + 2-8-4	17½″ × 26″ (4)	4′-7½″	2649	44.2	200	45 910	165-12-2	Garratt type maximum axle load 12-14-0
34	15A	1550–1557	8	1939	Vulcan	4-8-0	19½″ × 28″	5′-8″	2160	32.6	225	28 200	155-6-0	Four built with Caprotti valve gear
35	15B	1561–1590	30	1949	Vulcan	4-8-0	19½″ × 28″	5′-8″	2097	33.0	225	28 200	153-12-0	
36	BA	1-6, 17-22, 35-40	18	1906–07	N. British	2-8-0	19″ × 26″	4′-10″	1950	30.0	175	22 655	133-18-2	6 fitted with boilers ex-class 12B 1937-40
37	BB	451–462	12	1906–07	N. British	2-8-0	17″ × 24″	4′-4″	1176	21.0	175	18 674	99-12-0	2 fitted with Western Ry class 200 boilers 1935
38	BD	1032-35, 1044-48	9	1905–06	N. British	4-6-0	19″ × 26″	5′-7″	1524	24.0	175	19 612	101-11-0	
39	BE	2515-18, 2533-38, 2565-68	14	1904–15	N. British & Kerr Stuart	0-6-0 ST	16″ × 24″	4′-1″	903	15.0	160	16 050	39-5-3	
40	12M	330-42, 350, 360, 361-363-364	18	1921	Maffei, Cockerill & St. Pierre	4-6-2	19 11/16″ × 26 13/16″	5′-3″	2319	32.3	170	20 800	122-0-0	Ex-state Ry
41	14A	500–501	2	1926	Baldwin	2-10-2	22″ × 26″	4′-3″	3656	44.1	200	39 281	158-18-0	Ex-state Ry
42	75H	101–150	24	1922	Henschel	2-8-2	11 13/16″ × 17 5/16″	2′-7½″	902	14.0	170	10 440	50-2-0	Es-state Ry /5 cm. gauge
43	75B	1-6, 16-22	12	1922	Baldwin	2-8-2	11 13/16″ × 17 5/16″	2′-7½″	902	14.0	170	10 440	47-1-0	Ex-state Ry 75 cm. gauge

Notes (1) The diagrams have been traced from the official type sketch drawings
(2) Some of the total weights varied according to the type of tender fitted

Index